GREAT PICTURES
AND THEIR STORIES

How To Look At Pictures

"You must look at pictures studiously, earnestly, honestly. It will take years before you come to a full appreciation of art; but when at last you have it, you will be possessed of the purest, loftiest and most ennobling pleasures that the civilized world can offer you."

JOHN C. VAN DYKE.

ST.
A A
PRESS

GREAT PICTURES ⷮ THEIR STORIES

INTERPRETING MASTERPIECES TO CHILDREN

BY
KATHERINE MORRIS LESTER

BOOK NINE

ST. AUGUSTINE ACADEMY PRESS

This book was originally published in 1930
by Mentzer, Bush & Company.

This facsimile edition reprinted in 2024
with improved color images
by St. Augustine Academy Press.

ISBN: 978-1-64051-152-1

CONTENTS

Page

INDEX OF ILLUSTRATIONS IN GREAT PICTURES AND THEIR STORIES

FOREWORD

There is everywhere today an awakened interest in American art. The service our native painters have rendered in developing art in America is being more and more recognized and appreciated with the passing of the years. American art is being so emphasized by private collectors, dealers, exhibitors, and the leading art galleries that to be uninformed in regard to this, our national heritage, is indeed to be not fully abreast of the times.

In planning Book IX of this series it has been the primary aim of those selecting the artists and pictures to make it distinctly an "All-American" volume. A beginning is thus made in enabling our youthful students to form a correct valuation of the leaders in American art.

In the selection of artists ten established leaders in the various fields have been chosen. In the selection of pictures the aim has been to consider always the student's interest, and also to present pictures best suited to his comprehension.

In the earlier grades the interest in picture is largely in story, and in the emotional response to the beauty of color and pattern. Later this interest in story and color leads gradually to a further interest in HOW the story is told—the real ART of the picture. Thus the pupil begins to temper the emotional response of earlier years with a degree of understanding of those art elements which produce it.

In the high school the emphasis is placed on ART FORM or FINENESS OF DESIGN. The art elements, COLOR, LINE, and DARK AND LIGHT PATTERN, are carefully studied. The many possibilities of these art elements and their various effects are pointed out. The student is thus led to an appreciation of fine choices in color, line, and pattern. This greatly assists him further in his appreciation of the fine selections of color, line, and pattern made by all the great artists in their many and varied expressions of beauty.

This understanding, combined with the emotional

appeal, gives the student a background, leading him to an intelligent, hence a REAL APPRECIATION of beauty in the fine arts. It is this more complete interpretation of a work of art that imparts added interest to the study of masterpieces in the high school.

Each picture in this American series is followed by a brief sketch of the artist. This tends to familiarize the pupil with the peculiar niche which he occupies in American art.

The questions which follow the text will assist in developing an intelligent understanding of the art principles which underlie the production of all masterpieces. This method of approach will enable students to cultivate an appreciation of art in its most complete sense.

The MUSICAL SELECTIONS for the pictures have been chosen only with the thought of their EMOTIONAL CORRESPONDENCE to the picture. They have been graciously contributed by Eva G. Kidder, Director of Music, Peoria Public Schools. The author believes this to be a very valuable and enjoyable feature of the study program.

KATHERINE MORRIS LESTER.

ILLUSTRATED WITH REPRO-
DUCTIONS IN COLOR FROM
THE ORIGINAL MASTER-
PIECES, BY COURTESY OF
THE ART EXTENSION
SOCIETY OF NEW YORK.

JAMES WHITCOMB RILEY
John Herron Art Institute, Indianapolis

ARTIST: John Singer Sargent
SCHOOL: American
DATES: 1856-1925

JAMES WHITCOMB RILEY

"It's the songs ye sing
And the smiles ye wear
That's a makin' the sun shine everywhere."

If, as is well said, the chief glory of portrait painting is the revelation of character, then indeed is it true that the Sargent portrait of James Whitcomb Riley is a masterpiece. One sees in Mr. Sargent's painting the very qualities that made the success of Mr. Riley. Playing about the eyes and around the mouth of this beloved portrait are all the subtle shades of bubbling humor, wholesome fun, and kindly sympathy that made Riley, Riley. The pleasant face calls to mind the frequently repeated remark of his favorite nurse: "Now isn't that good. He looks as if he were just going to say something pleasant." Yes indeed, in that gentle countenance one sees again the lively imagination that gave to the world "The Raggety Man," "Little Orphant Annie" with its ever popular refrain,

"An' the gobbl-uns 'll git you
Ef you
Don't
Watch
Out,"

and many other lines of characteristic Riley quality.

True to his understanding of just what a portrait should be, the artist has seized upon the big characteristics, the outstanding features of Mr. Riley's personality, and placed them upon canvas. Ability to do this is the real test of a painter of portraits.

John Singer Sargent has come to be recognized as one of the great portrait painters of the modern world because he was able to do that very thing. Above all else he catches that "intangible something" which IS his subject, whether it be the pose of the head, the lift of the eyebrow, or the play of a sensitive countenance. The one thing that gave individuality, the essence of character, as he saw it, was grasped by the artist and made the dominant interest in the portrait. So here, in this beloved portrait of the poet of Indiana, one will not say it is the natural pose of the figure, with the arm thrown across the back of the chair, the slightly inclined head, or even the suggestion of gentle humor, that makes our portrait. Not any ONE of these, but taken altogether, they weave the perfect whole. They speak as plainly as words could tell the manner of man he was.

Notice how the artist has centered all the interest about the head. The rich, dark background serves to emphasize the contour and pose of the head, and brings out the fine flesh tones. The left side of the figure is well-nigh lost in the dark background, while by contrast, the line of the right shoulder and arm is emphasized by the gradually lightened background. The repetition of the flesh tones, toned off, in the two hands, carries the interest from the head to the hands and back again to the pleasant face of the poet.

Reducing the portrait to three values helps one to see how the artist has arranged his "lights," and how he has placed the figure on the canvas.

How simply the whole portrait is managed! The dark masses of the coat are laid on in a simple broad way with no effort whatever to show every little wrinkle, every little shadow. These great masses of dark are painted, it seems, simply to enframe the sensitive countenance. Notice how the crisp, snow-white tips of the collar enhance the flesh tones of the face, while the repetition, in the cuffs, only repeats this interest about the hands. Thus

13

the artist keeps every part of the portrait subordinate to the character expressed in the face of the poet.

In this way the artist has given to the world his portrait of Mr. Riley. Once when questioned about its resemblance to the poet, Mr. Sargent quietly replied, "It is the way I saw him."

Thus while interpreting the man as he did, the world recognizes in the portrait the character it had so long admired and loved. This alone is convincing proof of the ART quality imparted to the painting.

It was in the year 1900 that Mr. Riley gave a reading of his poems and generously donated the proceeds to the Indiana Art Association. The Association later invited the master painter, John Singer Sargent, who was then living in London, to paint the portrait of their poet-citizen. At this time Mr. Sargent was painting the portraits of many distinguished persons in England. Three years later, however, he came to America and fulfilled the long-cherished hope of the people of Indiana by painting this portrait of their most distinguished citizen. Today this painting hangs in one of the galleries of the John Herron Institute of Indianapolis. It is constantly visited not only by citizens of Indiana but by Riley's admirers from all parts of the world.

THE ARTIST.

While John Singer Sargent is recognized as a "man of many nations," he himself asserted that he was an American. Born in Italy of American parents, and living in Italy, France, England, Switzerland, Germany, and speaking fluently the languages of these countries, it is not surprising that he is considered a "citizen of the world."

Fortunate, indeed, was the artist to have been reared in the beauty-loving city of Florence. Twice blest indeed was he, not only in the place of his birth, but in the understanding sympathy of his parents. His mother was an accomplished painter in water colors, and she with the father fostered every little evidence of the young boy's budding genius.

No doubt the youthful John Sargent lived his life in much the same way as would any American boy fortunate enough to have his home in Florence. He roamed about the quaint streets of the city. These were the only streets he had known! He visited the grand palaces, once the homes of the most powerful families of Florence. He lingered as long as he liked before the great pictures painted by Raphael, Correggio, Titian, del Sarto, the great artists of all time. He saw over and over again the work of Michaelangelo. He was free to go whenever he wished to the old churches of Florence, where he saw again and again the work of the first great painters of the Renaissance. He was surrounded, you see, on all sides by the art treasures of this historic city. He constantly breathed an atmosphere permeated with this same feeling of beauty. These are opportunities which seldom come to one in a lifetime, and yet this was all a part of the everyday life of John Singer Sargent before he was out of his teens.

It was evidently the cherished hope of his parents that the lad should become an artist. His childish sketches aroused their highest anticipations. It is said that his mother frequently took the boy on sketching trips. She permitted him to "begin as many sketches as he liked," but made it a rule that "one of them must be finished." This incident alone goes to show the careful upbringing and guiding direction of the parents. When quite young the lad developed the happy faculty of seizing upon tricks of expression in the face, and carrying these out with an accuracy which augured much for his coming greatness as a portrait painter.

It was while still a youth that a little incident occurred that gave him great inspiration. His family was spending a summer in the Tyrol. A very distinguished figure in the art and literary world happened to be sojourning in the same place. This was the eminent painter and future president of the Royal Academy, Sir Frederick Leighton. He was a genial man. He could sing, dance, play, and tell a story with so much charm that he instantly won the heart of an audience. Young Sargent fell under his spell. One day when the Sargents were entertaining this distinguished gentleman, the young boy was induced, under protest, to bring out his drawings for their guest to examine. The artist scanned the sketches critically, very critically. The boy waited with bated breath. Finally, "Good," said the master, "I see you know how to draw a line," and then admonished, "Go on with your art, by all means."

What a spur this was to young Sargent's ambition! His face glowed with pleasure. He attacked his work with renewed vigor. By the time he was eighteen he had a collection of drawings which he hoped would at least bear witness to his ability. Whether they would proclaim him the artist he hoped to be the future would disclose.

Just then many ambitious American students were going to Paris for study. John Sargent, too, felt Paris calling. With his portfolio of drawings and accompanied by his father, he set out for the famous city. Once there, the next step of importance was to seek the advice of the brilliant young artist, Carolus Duran. It was with some trepidation that young Sargent watched this famous painter thumb through his sketches. Finally, it must have been with something of a shock, he heard him say: "Hum! You have much to unlearn!" Nevertheless he agreed to take the young man into his studio.

Sargent was serious minded and an earnest worker, and this, no doubt, together with his marked ability brought him steadily into greater favor with his teacher. Duran praised his work and constantly encouraged him. He recognized that Sargent had a style and individuality that was distinctly his own. Mr. Sargent took all that the brilliant French teacher had to give, but never for a moment imitated him. Though his practiced eye and hand gathered much, he was always original. He was soon recognized as a painter with a real future before him.

Later he and his brilliant teacher parted company. Sargent continued his travels and study. In Spain it was the simplicity and perfection of the works of Velasquez, the great Spanish master, that became to him an ideal.

While in Spain he painted one of his best known canvasses, "El Jaleo," which pictures a Spanish dancing girl with castanets, swaying in rhythmic dance to the music of several guitars. This painting is now in Fenway Court, Boston. It was bequeathed to the city in 1924 by Mrs. Isabella Stewart Gardiner, "for the education and enjoyment of the public forever."

By the time Mr. Sargent was thirty he was famous. Apparently all things came to him easily, wealth, success, fame. He was a reserved, quiet man, and never talked of his difficulties; consequently the world considered he had none. Yet it is true that Mr. Sargent was an indefatigable worker, a student, serious minded from the start. He was a severe critic of his own work, and would never allow anything to leave the studio until he was satisfied with it. Sometimes this meant the repainting of a portrait many, many times. He is known to have erased a head thirty or forty times before it met with his satisfaction.

In London, whither he went in 1884, he met with immediate recognition. To show her appreciation of his work, Queen Victoria offered him the rights of English citizenship, which he courteously declined.

In 1887 he visited America. His fame had preceded him, and upon reaching this country he was immediately besieged by fashionable families who desired to have their portraits painted.

Sargent has been called the greatest of modern portrait painters. Among the famous Americans who sat for him are Theodore Roosevelt, Woodrow Wilson, John D. Rockefeller, Augustus Saint Gaudens, James Whitcomb Riley, Charles W. Eliot, and other notables.

Though he excelled in portraiture, other works are equally famous. His well-known "Carmencita," the Spanish dancer, was purchased by the French government. Again, his happy interpretation of children in "Carnation, Lily, Lily Rose," is one of his superb pictures now in the Tate Gallery, London.

In 1890 Sargent's star attained its full magnitude. He received the commission to decorate the end walls of a hall in the Boston Public Library. This was a new field, that of mural decoration. As was his custom, Sargent bent all his energies to the accomplishment of this work. Five years later, when the first of these murals was in place, popular enthusiasm ran so high that a sufficient sum was immediately raised to complete the side panels connecting the end walls. These superb decorations, among them the celebrated "Frieze of the Prophets," stand today as a fitting memorial to the distinguished service of this eminent American, John Singer Sargent, "citizen of the world."

STUDY FOR APPRECIATION

1. What is the distinguishing quality of a portrait?

   What determines the ability of a portrait painter?

2. How does a portrait differ from a photograph?

3. Point out these qualities in this portrait.

4. Name characteristics of the poet which you read in the portrait.

5. Where has the artist placed his emphasis? How do you know?

   What is of secondary interest?

   How do you know?

6. Does the artist use color to give light? Does the artist use color to make pattern?

   Does the artist use chiefly color, or line, or strong contrasts of dark and light, to give art form to the portrait?

7. Who is the artist?

   How does he rank as a painter?

   Why is he called a "citizen of the world"?

8. Name other famous works of this master.

9. Where is this portrait? Do you like it? Why?

Related Music:............................*Little Orphant Annie*
(Reading recorded with music)

THE MILL POND
Art Institute, Chicago

ARTIST: George Inness
SCHOOL: American
DATES: 1824-1910

THE MILL POND

In the Art Institute of Chicago is one of the finest collections in existence of the work of a single artist. Here in the "Inness Gallery" are twenty-one famous paintings of George Inness, one of the greatest of American painters, the "Father of American Landscape."

In this rare collection of pictures one sees the whole range of this painter's work, that of his early period, and that of later days. Among those of his more mature years is the rich, colorful canvas, "The Mill Pond."

Dimly seen on the far edge of a shady, placid pool stands an old mill. This drowsy pool, spread as a mirror before the old mill, is the typical mill pond, green, sluggish, and slow. Hugging the water's edge and massed high above the old mill is the thick foliage of motionless trees, their reds, yellows, and warm greens suggesting the dull languor that hangs over such a pond in late summer.

Without doubt it was this very "FEELING" in the scene that impressed the artist, for it is this that he has put upon canvas. True, it is a real scene, with much richness of color, but above and beyond this is the "mood" or "spirit" of the place which the artist has interpreted.

In his later years Mr. Inness painted

especially with this thought in mind. In his own writings he says: "The purpose of the painter is simply to reproduce in other minds the impression which a scene has made on him." Further he says that details in a picture should be elaborated only enough to reproduce the impression which the artist wishes to make.

These words are especially interesting in the study of "The Mill Pond," for here the detail is largely omitted, and the scene painted in a mass of low, rich tones of color.

One can scarcely see the old mill on the far side of the pond. Its outlines are lost in the surrounding foliage. The warm greens and tawny yellows of the distant trees melt into the placid pool and its dim reflections. Nearer, the rich, warm red of the big tree is patterned against the mass of foliage, clouds, and sky. Though its color is softened and its outline merged into surrounding color, its form is strongly and clearly defined. Above, its rounded top is set against the deep grayed-blue of the sky. Below, it is rooted in the green foreground. Notice particularly the fine color contrast in the red tree and green foreground. It seems that all other color in the painting has been merged together as a setting for this splendid tree-form at the edge of the mill pond.

The light coming from above falls upon the lone figure in the little boat, the gnarled logwood, and the scattered foliage on the near edge of the pool; then it mirrors itself, yellow-green, under the big tree.

Reducing the picture to three values helps one to see the beauty and simplicity of pattern.

Thus the artist has shown only the big red tree and the lighted objects as accents in his picture. Altogether the picture becomes a mass of rich, warm color, suggesting the close, languorous atmosphere which hangs about an old mill and its pond. It is the poetry in the artist's thought and the magic of his brush that make us feel the drowsy atmosphere, that help us see the mellowed color, that bring to us the odor of green things, still water, and old woods.

How glowing is the color! Grayed yellows, yellow-greens, greens, reds, and blue! Though it is all subdued color, it is so artistically placed that the painting takes on the form of a well-chosen pattern. Though there is much in the scene, all has been veiled, and only that color and form elaborated which will create the impression the painter desired, and convey the atmosphere or "feeling" of the place.

Thus it is that the artist interprets nature; thus it is that this REAL scene, through the seeing eye of the painter, has been rendered artistically. The glowing, poetic nature of the artist has transformed the REAL into the IDEAL.

THE ARTIST

It was a little less than a hundred years ago, when Newark, New Jersey, was only a village, that George Inness was trying to find his niche in the world. In this little town the elder Inness had opened a grocery store, and made George chief clerk, in the hope that this might start the lad on a successful business career. George was a tall, slender youth, with pale face and dreamy eyes. He was more the dreamer than the alert business man, and seemed strangely out of place behind the counter selling cheese, butter, and eggs.

George, however, needed no help to discover he was out of his sphere. He was quite aware of it. Business lagged. "I am afraid George will never be a successful business man," sighed the despairing father. It was only after the father was convinced that George was hopeless in the grocery, or in fact in any other business, that he permitted him to follow his bent. After due deliberation the best teacher available was secured, and the lad was placed under his supervision. So earnestly did the boy apply himself that soon the teacher acknowledged that he could teach him nothing more. Then it was that the youth, studying and working out his own theories, began the long series of experiments which led to his great success in later years.

Landscape seemed to be his particular field. He covered his canvases with wide-spreading country, picturing trees, hills, dales, streams, and other details, worked out with truth-telling accuracy. In fact these early paintings were as near photographic likenesses as it was possible to make them. He was never quite satisfied with these, however, always feeling that there was something just beyond which he must grasp.

It is one of the remarkable features of the

work of George Inness that he learned from no master. Instead he began with these exact reproductions of nature, and through his own effort and reflection attained to a higher form of artistic expression.

One day he was attracted to some prints of the old masters which lay in an engraver's window. He was fascinated with them, and bought one for study. There was a bigness and simplicity about it that appealed to him. He carried the print about with him, studying it and comparing it with nature as she really is. "Gradually," he says, "the light began to dawn."

After much travel and study abroad, we find the lesson taught in the little print having its effect. Detail is now omitted and only those essentials are elaborated which add to the artistic interpretation of nature. In his own writings he says: "The impression of a scene as a unit is lost when we see simply an array of external things, which may be very cleverly painted and look very real, but which do not make an artistic picture."

"Peace and Plenty" of the Metropolitan Museum is an excellent example of the painter's early manner. The artistry of his mature style is seen in, "The Mill Pond", "Early Morning", "Tarpon Springs", and many others in the collection of the Art Institute of Chicago.

STUDY FOR APPRECIATION

1. What is your first impression of this painting?
2. Has the artist painted a REAL scene?
   How does it differ from a photograph?
3. Has the artist used color as it is in nature?
   Is it "warm" or "cool"?
   Is it closely harmonized or strongly contrasted?
   Does the color help to interpret the picture? How?
4. Make a sketch showing arrangement of picture plan.
   Where does the interest center?
   Has the arrangement of color helped to center the interest here?
5. What gives pattern to the picture?
6. What element emphasized in the artist's writings is observed here?
7. Who is the artist?
   To what period of work does this painting belong?
   What are the characteristics of this period?
8. Name other famous works.
9. How does the artist rank as a landscapist?

Related Music: AUTUMN ....*Moskowski*
SYMPHONY NO. 5 IN C MINOR
—Andante ....*Beethoven*
ADAGIO CANTABILE FROM
SONATA PATHETIQUE..........
Beethoven

29

NORTHEASTER

Metropolitan Museum, New York

ARTIST: Winslow Homer
SCHOOL: American
DATES: 1836-1910

NORTHEASTER

A tumultuous sea!
Crested breakers rolling,
Swishing,
Swirling,
Cloud spray dashing high!
This—A NORTHEASTER!

The rearing, plunging "white horses" of old King Neptune never rode to shore with greater dash and spirit than does the tumultous surf of Winslow Homer's sea. Movement is everywhere. The sea surges. It heaves and halts. It rises and falls. The salt spray is dashed against the rocks. It forms a cloud. It fills the air. The opalescent foam of the breakers rides upon the surging billows. In the deep trough of the sea there is a swish and swirl of counter currents. Never has the agitation of the sea, lashed into fury by the elements, been so dramatically pictured!

Few knew the sea as did Winslow Homer. Living high up on the rock-bound coast of Maine, he studied the sea in all its moods. He knew the calm, with the low lapping of the waters. He knew quite as well the storm, as its fury lashed the great immovable rocks.

In this famous painting, "Northeaster," he pictures the power of moving water. How little there is in the picture! Above, only a stretch of the overcast sky; in the foreground,

31

a bit of rocky coast; beyond, the swelling re-
sistless sea.

One can easily understand why there are
few painters of the sea. To the uninitiated
there is much of monotony about a vast stretch
of water. But to the painter who knows the
sea and its moods, there are possibilities
forever hidden from the unseeing crowd.

See the play of movement and changing
color pictured in the turbulent sea! There is

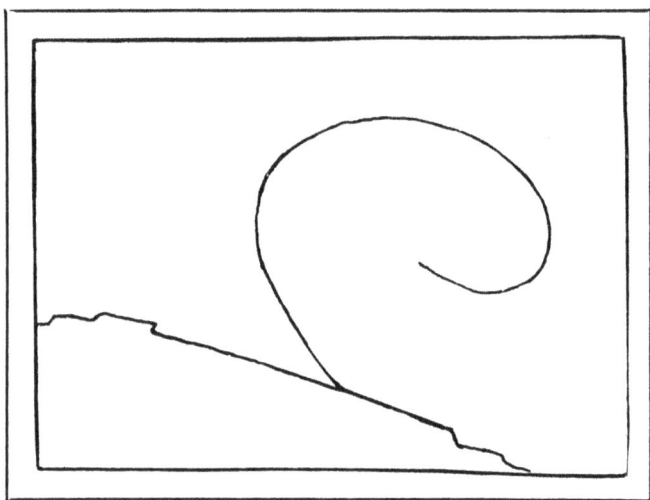

The line of movement carries the eye over the picture, and
gives design-form to the composition.

no monotony here. Variety in both form and
color give pattern to the composition. Notice
how the artist leads into the picture. The eye

sweeps up the rocky coast taking in the cloud spray, and then unconsciously wheels, in one big sweeping curve, over and under the crested foam of the distant billow. In this way the artist makes the principal movement of the composition cover the picture. This gives unity to the design-form of the picture.

Just as a horizontal movement gives tranquillity and repose; as a vertical movement gives dignity and strength; so here the diagonal movement increases the feeling of motion and power. This same diagonal movement is constantly repeated in the picture pattern. Note the formation of the coast, the long diagonal lines add to the force of the movement. Again, the delicate tracery of sea foam, as it moves here and there over the surface, forms its strongest masses in direct line with the diagonal movement of the picture. In this way the artist expresses a rhythmic pattern of movement which is immediately felt, though one may be unconscious of the art structure of the composition.

In color there is again the same feeling for art form. The great mass of cloud, brown in the foreground is repeated, toned off, in the distant sky. Thus a balance of color interest is secured. Note, too, the vibrant quality of these brown color tones. You will observe that they are made of many colors. The pigments have been so chosen and mingled that the result gives a vibrating effect, or as it is sometimes said, an effect of "singing color." Between the two dark masses of brown is the turbulent sea of green. Yes, a sea of green! The eye is carried from the delicate opalescent tints in the sea foam to the light and middle tones and then down to the darkest greens in the shadows. This range of beautiful tone combined with the pattern of foam on the waves gives this area of sea a beauty seldom pictured in paintings of moving water.

Note the contrast of brown foreground with the cloud spray. The dark mass brings out the subtle color painted into the moving spray. Further the darkened under-portion of the spray helps to give rounded form and volume to the cloud. This softening of the under part is in marked contrast to the clear-cut edge of the whites silhouetted against the dark sky. To further emphasize the whites of the cloud spray, the artist has darkened the sky following the edge of the light mass, and carried the dark tone across the distant horizon as well. This causes the sky to recede still more, thus giving the illusion of greater distance. One is led to feel that the rolling, restless sea goes far beyond the confines of the canvas.

Though we may note all these details in the design-form of the picture, the painting is, first of all, a great interpretation of the power and grandeur of the sea. It is, indeed, a picture of the real sea expressed in magnificent simplicity. The artist, however, has expressed his picture of the real in the form of design or pattern, and it is this element that gives artistic quality to the painting, placing it among the first of great pictures of the sea. It is Winslow Homer's masterly portrayal of the "spirit" of the sea in all its moods that has won for him first place among American marine painters.

THE ARTIST

Winslow Homer was born with the love of the sea in his blood. In fact, the artist was proud to claim a real pirate among his ancestors. For generations his family had been seafaring people. His father was a direct descendant of the famous John Homer who crossed the Atlantic in his own boat in the middle of the sixteenth century.

With such a heritage it is not surprising that Winslow Homer found his most complete expression in pictures of the sea. The storm, the ruggedness of life at sea, the power of moving water, the great elemental forces playing upon the deep, these were the moods he chose to interpret.

Born in Boston in 1836, Winslow Homer

spent his early boyhood in and about that city. When he was six years of age his parents moved to Cambridge, where he entered school. Here he became the despair of his teachers, for instead of keeping his books tidy and clean he covered their margins with pictures. Reprove the lad as they would, his books still continued to be dotted with fanciful sketches. Young Homer remained in Cambridge enjoying the free, outdoor life of a New England village, and in particular his favorite sport of fishing. At eighteen his future career began to take definite form.

Fortunate indeed it was for the boy that as a lad his father had lent a kindly ear to his ambitions. The talent which Winslow had so early displayed greatly interested his father. Now as plans looking toward a vocation for the boy began to mature, the parent, wise man that he was, looked about for something in which the young man's talent could be employed.

"How would you like to learn engraving?" he asked.

"I believe I should like it," replied the boy.

While plans such as these were being considered, his father happily succeeded in placing him as apprentice in a lithographer's shop in Cambridge. Though not enthusiastic about the work itself the lad realized it was an excellent training, just the training in craftsmanship which he needed; so he went to work with a will.

He spent these early years in the lithographer's shop, putting all his effort into learning as much as he could. Indeed, so skilful did he become in drawing and designing that in the short space of two years he was given much original work to do. Some of the important work of this period was the designing of title pages for sheet music. By and by young Homer resolved to give all his time to his chosen work. He left the lithograph shop and went to New York City. There he set up a studio of his own, and began the business of illustrating. Among the drawings of this period were those accepted by the New York house of Harper and Brothers. This recognition by so popular a paper as Harper's Weekly insured his success.

In the midst of his success, however, Winslow Homer was always a student. As time went on the young man realized more and more his need for greater preparation, more schooling in art. Consequently he began studying with a well-known French teacher. Later, his evenings were spent in the night classes of the National Academy of Design.

By and by came the Civil War. People wanted to know in graphic form what was going on at the front. Illustrations were in demand. Harper Brothers cast about for the right man for the work. They settled upon Winslow Homer.

Homer was delighted with the prospect of going to war. His boyish enthusiasm at once settled the question. He packed his belongings, and started across the Potomac with the first regiment of volunteers in 1861.

During several months at the front his sketches were regularly sent to the paper. Every phase of camp life, humorous and otherwise, was pictured in these early drawings. Upon his return to New York City, certain of his war experiences furnished suggestions for a number of paintings in oil.

At the close of the war Homer was thirty years old. He was fast making a name for himself. In 1864 he held his first exhibition, showing at this time his canvas called "Prisoners at the Front." This was a war picture which stirred the patriotic interest of all who saw it. It made a very great impression, which brought still wider recognition to the artist. During the same year his interest in water color drawing, in which he was a master, led to the organization of the American Water Color Society. Though by this time his work had brought him fame, there awaited him an even greater day.

It was not until Winslow Homer heard the "call of the sea" that he became the great painter that he is. True to his ancestral love of the sea he found his way to its shore. There on the rugged coast of Maine, at Prout's Neck, high among the rocks, he built a dwelling place for himself. Here, secluded from the haunts of civilization, he lived alone with the sea. He studied every phase of the calm and the storm. He knew the grandeur of the sea, its movement, its sublimity. It is this elemental power and grandeur that distinguishes his later pictures.

Homer knew not only the sea, but also the people who live by the sea. In his earliest pictures there is always this human interest. In these pictures the sea is merely a background creating an atmosphere for the figures, whose life he knew so well. Later however these familiar forms gradually take a smaller place in his pictures, until in his more mature period he chose to paint only the power and grandeur of the sea.

"Northeaster" is considered one of the greatest of the artist's great pictures. It hangs in the superb collections of the Metropolitan Museum of Art, New York City. Other museums and galleries of the country are considered fortunate in possessing the works of this famous marine painter. "High Cliff, Coast of Maine", in the National Gallery, Washington, D. C.; "The Gale", in the Art Museum, Worcester, Mass.; "The Wreck", in the Carnegie Institute, Pittsburgh; and "Fog Warning", in the Boston Museum of Fine Arts, are among his most famous works. The Art Institute of Chicago is the proud possessor of a collection of Homer's water color drawings.

Not only in his own country but in Europe as well the merit of Mr. Homer's work is acknowledged. In 1900 he sent several paintings to the Universal Exposition at Paris. There his work was accorded high honors. He was awarded a gold medal, and one of his pictures was purchased by the French government.

Of all American artists Winslow Homer probably owes least to outside influence. He was untaught by foreign art, but developed his own thoroughly individual style. Moreover he found his subjects in the grandeur of his own New England coast. For this reason America has come to look upon him as in every respect distinctly American.

In 1900 an exhibition of American art was held in Germany. A writer on this occasion, greatly impressed by the striking individuality and power of Homer's work, pointedly asked,—"Can we find any sign of a national art in America?" He then answered promptly and simply, "Winslow Homer."

STUDY FOR APPRECIATION

1. Is this a REAL scene?
   What feeling about the sea has the artist interpreted?
2. What gives this picture art quality?
3. Is the general movement of the composition vertical, horizontal, or diagonal?
   What effect does this give?
4. Make a sketch showing the principal line of movement.
5. Point out rhythmic movement in the painting.
6. Has the artist used color as it is in nature?
   Is it warm or cold?
   Is it strongly contrasted or closely harmonized?
7. What gives volume to the cloud spray?
8. Why has the sky been darkened along the cloud's edge?
   How does the darkened horizon add to the picture?
9. Who is the artist?
   How does he rank as a marine painter?
10. Name other famous works of this master.

Related Music: THE STORM FROM WM.
TELL ...._Rossini_
OVERTURE — The F l y i n g
Dutchman ...._Wagner_

THE WHISTLING BOY
Cincinnati Museum of Art

ARTIST: Frank Duveneck
SCHOOL: American
DATES: 1848-1919

THE WHISTLING BOY.

"The Whistling Boy" by Frank Duveneck is one of the best loved pictures in the Cincinnati Museum of Art. Here is a masterpiece by an American artist who is acclaimed the "greatest talent of the brush of this generation."

These words spoken by John Singer Sargent express concisely and graphically the peculiar genius of this modern master. It is his brush work, his expressive use of paint, that makes him a leader in American art.

Never did Mr. Duveneck spend much time in perfecting a carefully finished charcoal or crayon drawing as a foundation for paint. On the contrary as soon as the outlines were only roughly suggested, he quickly covered his canvas with paint and proceeded to model in pigment.

"The Whistling Boy" is a masterpiece painted in this way. Notice the brush work on the clothes, the old apron, and the shirt. Here you will observe many colors have been laid on, and then modeled in such a way that a depth and richness of texture results. This is an effect attained joyfully, not by following outlines of drawing, but instead by spontaneity of expression in brush and paint, combined with a FEELING for rich, harmonious color. Notice, too, that both the color and handling of paint in the clothes are completely subordinate to the color and detail of the head. Mr. Duveneck seemed to know just how far to go in the various parts of a picture to lead up to the "center of interest." The somber color harmony of many of his pictures is relieved by just the necessary luminous color which emphasizes and reveals the center of interest.

True, the figure and clothes of the boy are interesting, depicting as they do a little urchin of the streets. But it is the head, the eyes, the expression, that hold the attention. Here is the high luminous color. This IS the boy,—the whistling boy of Frank Duveneck!

Note the solidity of the head, an effect attained by modeling the paint. Note the marvelously fresh color tones. With his usual skill in modeling and his feeling for color, he has succeeded in interpreting in picture the confident, care-free, whistling boy of today and yesterday.

See the towsled hair, the frank, open, somewhat dreamy eye, the childish nose, the rosy mouth! Notice the posture of the arm and hand. He may be looking at you with those dark languorous eyes, but his thought is fixed on the tune that he whistles. He is proud of the way he carries the tune!

In further studying the painting one will

observe the simple masses of color in the clothes and their color value as well. There are the dark greens, the tawny yellows, and lighter gray-whites. These masses, very simple, emphasize by contrast the glowing color and details of the head. Again, in the composition you will notice a rhythmic diagonal movement in the darks and lights of the pattern. The mass of black hair moves diagonally across the light forehead. This is in line with the chin and side face against the dark neck. It is again repeated in the V-shaped neckline of the light shirt, the dark green vest, the tawny apron, and still again in the lowest edge of the apron, where the fold is made by catching it in with the belt. The arm and hand, you will also notice, fall in with this same diagonal movement. Opposite, the arm and hand, together with whatever it may be that he carries, is submerged in an indefinite mass of color tones which sustain the harmony of the dark, rich color of the composition. Do you notice that the dark hand, upward turned, leads directly to the bright luminous countenance?

Thus it is, through carefully selected color values and rhythmic repetition of color masses that the artist has given pattern to his composition. These are the art qualities that one unconsciously feels when viewing the picture.

These are the elements together with the un-matched excellence of the artist's manner that make this painting a masterpiece in the realm of the arts.

Reducing the picture to four values helps one to see the large simple areas which make the pattern.

Frank Duveneck's "Whistling Boy" was painted in 1872, when the artist was twenty-four years old. From the first it has constantly received high tribute, until today it is recognized as his most famous picture. You will notice that it is signed with the artist's unique monogram, and followed by, "Munich, 1872."

THE ARTIST

Frank Duveneck is often called "the painter's painter." This is because, above all others, it is the painter alone who can best understand and appreciate his work.

True it is that the world is not so familiar with the works of Frank Duveneck. This, however, is because his paintings were not generally accessible to the public, and moreover were best understood only by students of painting. The art world today, however, recognizes that Frank Duveneck is one of the greatest painters this country has produced.

Some seventy years ago, if one had stopped in the little town of Covington, Kentucky, on the Ohio River opposite Cincinnati, he would have found there an old monastery where the brothers were making altars for Catholic churches. Here he would doubtless have noticed a young flaxen-haired boy who was modeling figures, gilding them, and in other ways making himself generally useful. This lad was none other than the youthful Frank Duveneck. In this old monastery at Covington, helping the brothers in filling their orders, he began a career which carried him to the foremost rank among American painters.

It was when Frank Duveneck was a very, very little boy that he first showed signs of talent. He took childish delight in playing with the soft clay which he found on the bank of the river. It was great fun going up and down the street taking impressions of the highly polished door-plates of the neighbors' houses. Little did he know that these first efforts in clay were prophetic of great achievements.

It was, however, the employment given him in the old monastery at Covington that constantly stimulated his genius. Without much training, he here began to paint, model, carve and decorate. When he was about eighteen a German decorator, having work in a Cincinnati church, engaged the young man as his assistant. Under the guidance of this German craftsman young Duveneck developed so rapidly that he became exceedingly valuable to his employer. In later years Mr. Duveneck always referred to this work as an important part of his artistic training.

It was in 1870, when young Duveneck was twenty-two years old, that he was urged to go to Munich for further study. So great a part did this artistic city of southern Germany play in his development, that the names Duveneck and Munich are always associated.

During his first year in Munich the young artist won most of the prizes of the Academy.

At that time he painted a series of portraits upon which his fame rests. During the second year he painted his most famous picture,—"The Whistling Boy."

During his years as a student in Munich it was the work of the Dutch masters that influenced him most. His favorite among them was Frans Hals. Mr. Duveneck himself was of Dutch descent, and perhaps inherited something of the spirit and temper of the Dutch masters. It is said that he often took his pictures to the gallery of Munich and set them, for study and comparison, beside those of the Dutch painters. Today Mr. Duveneck's paintings are frequently likened to those of the famous Dutch masters. The Dutch painters showed a preference for rich warm browns, reds, and yellows. Because Mr. Duveneck favored these same tones, it is often remarked that in his pictures he has given us "the brown sauce of the old masters."

We are better able to understand and appreciate the "dark tones" of Mr. Duveneck's work, however, when we realize that he was painting at a period just preceding the introduction, by other artists, of gay sunlight and color. These artists recorded their impressions rather than attempting to give literal reproductions. For this reason they were called IMPRESSIONISTS. Strange as it may seem the impressionists had no great effect upon Mr. Duveneck's art. He still kept his own masterful style.

Mr. Duveneck was the first to dispense with the carefully drawn and shaded charcoal study as a foundation for paint. Instead he taught his pupils to block in the large masses, which gave the solid construction of head and torso, then to proceed to model in paint. It was this handling of a subject, particularly this MODELING IN PAINT, which gave that character to his work which is so often described as "purely Duveneck."

It was while living in Munich, in 1878, that his great popularity as a teacher led him to organize classes for young and ambitious American boys studying abroad. Under his inspiring leadership, and studying as they went, they traveled about Italy, painting in Florence, Venice, and other interesting places. They became very popular, and everywhere they went were known as the "Duveneck boys." In this group was John W. Alexander, who later became a painter of distinction.

Strange as it may seem after attaining such prominence in his art, Mr. Duveneck chose to give his time to further teaching. He returned to America, going to Cincinnati, and interested himself in developing a museum of art. He divided his time between painting and teaching, also advising in all artistic matters relating to the museum. Later, after the museum had become a reality, he occupied the attic as one of his studios. There he accumulated rolls of old canvases that he had painted in Europe. One day he determined to rid the attic of this accumulation, and prepared to burn them. A friend intervened. Gradually with careful work the canvases were flattened, stretched, framed, and hung in the museum. Mr. Duveneck was greatly interested, fully realizing the help these canvases would be to students. He later presented as a gift to the museum his entire collection of paintings, "for the benefit, particularly, of students of art in Cincinnati." This collection has now become a permanent memorial exhibition of his work.

Though never seeking distinction, and of a quiet and reserved disposition, Mr. Duveneck received many honors. At the Panama-Pacific Exposition held in San Francisco in 1915, he was one of twelve American artists to be given an entire room in the Art Palace. More than this, however, was the great distinction he received from the Jury of Awards of the Exposition. A commemorative medal was especially designed and presented to him in appreciation of his great service, as a teacher, to American art.

In the "Duveneck Room" at this exposition, "The Whistling Boy" was one of the outstanding pictures. "The Turkish Page", also a masterpiece, received a great deal of attention. That painting is especially distinguished by the simplicity, truth, and charm in the rendering of various materials, such as yellow feathers, leopard skin, a cuckatoo, metal, fruit, rich hangings, and living flesh.

"The Turkish Page" is now in the Pennsylvania Academy of Fine Arts, Philadelphia; "The Whistling Boy" is in the Cincinnati Museum of Art.

Among the most valued of the artist's own works in the Cincinnati Museum of Art is the original plaster cast for the exquisitely wrought memorial to Mrs. Duveneck, who died in Florence, Italy. The bronze memorial was set in place in Florence. A marble replica was later placed in the Boston Museum of Fine Arts. The Metropolitan Museum of Fine Arts possesses a bronze cast, and other leading collections in our country are proud in their ownership of reproductions of this beautiful American work.

The last notable work of Mr. Duveneck was a mural decoration, completed in 1910 and given to the Cathedral at Covington as a memorial to his mother.

STUDY FOR APPRECIATION

1. Would you classify this picture as story-telling, based on nature, or imaginative?
2. How does it differ from a photograph?
3. Where is the emphasis? Why?
   How has emphasis been secured?
   How has subordination of other parts been secured?
4. Are the colors closely related or strongly contrasted?
5. Point out and name the color values.
6. Does the picture show pattern?
   Explain in detail.
   Make a pencil sketch showing composition.
7. Name the art elements which make the painting a masterpiece.
8. Who is the artist?
   For what is he especially noted?
9. Do you see any evidence of his peculiar style in this picture? What?
10. Do you think the manner of painting is suited to the subject? Why?
11. Do you like the painting? Why?
    Name other of his famous works.
12. What is the meaning of "the brown sauce of the old masters?"

Related Music: SPRING VOICES..................*Strauss*
(Whistling solo)

MEN OF THE DOCKS
National Gallery, London

ARTIST: George Wesley Bellows
SCHOOL: American
DATES: 1882-1925

MEN OF THE DOCKS

Among artists of modern times the name of George Wesley Bellows is written large. To him is accorded the distinction of being a unique figure in modern American art.

In this painting, "Men of the Docks", true to his native inclination, Mr. Bellows has chosen a theme charged with the spirit and activity of the modern world. Under the brilliance of a radiant sunlight the innumerable details of the scene have fallen into large simple masses of light and dark. The modern city skyline, with its row upon row of skyscrapers and its rising clouds of smoke and vapor, have been so delightfully simplified that they only suggest, but that most effectively, the throbbing activity of our world of today. At the same time this treatment serves as a purposeful background to the workers, distinctly seen in the foreground.

From our point of vantage out on the dock we may view at leisure this scene, which so captivated the artist's fancy that he immediately set it upon canvas. There, in the dull gray distance, are the skyscrapers, masses of towering strength. A little nearer their strongly marked shadows give vertical accents to the colossal group. To the right is the ocean greyhound with its sweeping upper deck, its bridge, and towering stack. Beside it the saucy little tug, sending up continuous puffs of whirling vapor from its black cylindrical throat, lends its suggestion of restless power to the scene. Opposite is the old warehouse, so typical of the buildings that fringe the water's edge.

Observe how the whole scene falls into large shapes of dark and light, with detail omitted. Note the simplicity with which the scene is composed. To the right, the blue-gray bulk of the liner with its band of orange carries back to the throbbing city front. To the left the perspective lines of the dark warehouse, and the sharp edge of the light central mass lead alike to this same center of activity. It is only for a moment, however, that our interest remains here, for immediately the broad expanse of lighted area through the center carries us down, on past the puffing tug, to the foreground and its workers. Here are the men of the docks!

It is by no mere chance that the painter has grouped these workers more as a mass than as individuals. By so doing he suggests far more forcefully the strength and concentrated power of this group. Moreover you will observe that these men are not bending to their labor; they are not engaged in actual hard work. On the contrary, these rugged figures stand with heads up, looking about them, as if interested in the situation. Observe that their upright and stalwart forms repeat the vertical accents of the painting. The artist has thus given added force to this feeling of power in the composition.

Note further that in this group the artist repeats the color tones of his picture. True these same grays, blues, and browns of the painting have taken on an added depth and richness of color in the clothes of the workmen. This, however, as the artist intended, gives accent and force to the center of interest.

To the right of the group the two brawny horses, continuing as they do the light tone of the center, are a note of balance to the opposite light area. Their heavy forms give an added touch of reserve power to this foremost group. The broken patches of light in the very front of the picture serve as a foil to unify the pattern of light.

Thus it is that this modern painter brings his artistic sense to play upon the sun-lighted scene, reducing it to simple masses of form and color. This treatment tells the story far more effectively than would the introduction of many realistic details. This ability to reduce the complexity of such a scene to so simple a rendering recalls the emphatic statement of Mr. Whistler: "It is not the

person or thing painted that is of consequence, but the WAY IT IS PAINTED." So
in this picture, it is the WAY the artist saw
the picture and the simplicity with which he
interpreted its pattern that gives distinction.
This is indeed the ART of the picture!

"Men of the Docks" breathes forth the
characteristic spirit of the thriving, pulsing
waterfront of the great city of the twentieth
century!

Pattern reduced to simple lines leading into the picture and
carrying down to the mass of figures in the foreground—the
"center of interest."

THE ARTIST

No artist of modern times has been more popular with young people than George Wesley Bellows. He painted the things that young people like. His work is filled with the strong virile quality that appeals to youth. He was gay and enthusiastic, even spectacular, in the way he painted.

Fancy a prize ring with the subjects "Dempsey-Firpo", or "Ringside Seats" and the motley crowd that hugs the pugilists' platform! Again there is "Riverfront", picturing a mass of midsummer humanity, stripped, and ready for a plunge; again "Forty-two Kids", as many youngsters diving, swimming, and sunning themselves on a rickety old raft at the water's edge. Then again he passes from the teeming life of the docks to the beautiful home, with its lovely wife and children. Such is the range of interest of this versatile painter.

It is said that the artist's love of the pencil and brush was born with him. In his earliest years in kindergarten at Columbus, Ohio, where he was born, he was known as the "little artist." It seemed then as natural for him to draw as it was to breathe. In his school days he showed a liking for music and athletics. Later as a boy at college he "made" the baseball team and soon became a leader in that sport. He spent his vacations in illustrating and cartooning for the pages of the Ohio State Journal.

Art, music, athletics, these were what interested him most. Art and music came easily, athletics was more difficult, consequently he gave most of his attention to sport. He soon played baseball so well that he was urged to become a professional. By this time, however, he had made up his mind to paint. He declined the offer of professional ball playing and went forth to study seriously the art of pencil and brush.

Just then, for the public was watching with interest the progress of George Bellows, artist and sportsman, a news article appeared in which "Spurning a Career on the Diamond," was the startling headline. Then followed the story of how a certain young man was throwing away a rare opportunity in the field of sport to follow instead the doubtful career of an artist. In after years when talking with friends it is said that the now famous painter often referred to his love of this sport. "You know," he would say with an engaging smile, "I used to play baseball."

All through his art his love of the sport element is seen both in his choice of subjects and in the vigor and spontaneity of his work. Activity and movement characterize most of his subjects. When, however, among his many canvases one finds quiet and serenity it shows a poetic side of the artist that his energetic handling never reveals. Someone has said that had Mr. Bellows lived, for he died at the early age of forty-four, he would, no doubt, have combined with his strength of technique the charm and sweetness that come with maturity.

For three years Mr. Bellows studied with Robert Henri, a teacher who exercised a great influence upon American art. Bellows must have imbibed much of his teacher's feeling about the manner and mission of artistic expression. Henri used to say to his students, "Don't take me as an authority. I am simply expressing a very personal point of view . . . Find out what you really like if you can. Find out what is really important to you. Then sing your song. You will have something to sing about, and your whole heart will be in the singing. When a man is full up with what he is talking about, he handles such language as he has with a mastery unusual to him, and it is at such times that he learns language."

Mr. Bellows found what he liked. He never painted anything that did not deeply interest him, and more, he sang his song in a color and form of his own choosing. From his versatile brush came a surprisingly varied assortment. In circus riders and polo players, in the faces of gentle women and children, and in quiet nature settings he found an equal opportunity for his brilliant recordings of light and shade, color and mass. So new, so different, so vital was his art that he was easily recognized as a unique leader in the field of modern painting. Before Mr. Bellows was thirty many museums had honored him with a place upon their walls. When he passed away in January, 1925, he was represented in art collections in all parts of the country.

With the artist's death the art world recognized a great loss. In the flood of praise poured forth at this time it was constantly reiterated that George Bellows was exceptionally the "American painter." Speaking of Mr. Bellows as "one of the vital factors in the art of today," the New York Herald Tribune declared, "he had reality in his work and the power that goes with gusto . . . to his strong young vision the stuff of our national life made a vivid appeal and he responded with the eager spirit of a craftsman who was also a sportsman . . . his art flowed out of a wholesome robust nature." The Philadelphia Ledger regarded him as "distinctly American" in that "superlative gift of imagination." It also stated, "It has often been argued that America has done far less in literature and in music, to say nothing of the other arts, than might have been expected. But this does not hold true of American achievement in painting. The American painters of international repute make a long list. More than this, too, their work is truly native. It has the American atmosphere. Bellows was one of a noble band of brothers in art." Robert Henri, his well-known teacher paid the following tribute to his student and friend: "George Bellows, had he lived, would have gone on with continued success, mounting higher and higher in his ability as an artist, gaining universal approval as an artist and a man."

One can scarcely speak of the work of George Bellows without calling to mind his remarkable skill in lithography. This is the art of making a drawing on stone so that ink impressions can be taken from it. It is an art not so much practiced now as at an earlier date. In this Mr. Bellows was a devoted and accomplished master.

In October, 1925, the Metropolitan Museum of Art bestowed upon this painter the greatest honor within its power. This was an exhibition of his paintings and lithographs. It was known as the George Bellows Memorial Exhibition.

Among the artist's familiar later works, "Eleanor, Joan, and Ann," portraits showing an understanding of youth and age was awarded a medal of the first class at the International Exhibition at Pittsburgh in 1922. One of the most artistic memorials of the world is his great canvas, "Edith Cavell." This picture is recognized as the expression of a vivid imagination acting under the pressure of a great dramatic moment. "The Crucifixion of Christ," a large painting exhibited in 1924, the year preceding his death, brought a storm of criticism, but now seems destined to go down to posterity as one of his greatest achievements. All the work of Mr. Bellows possesses marked American quality. It has been said that if one of his pictures were hung in the Paris salon it might dimly suggest to a Frenchman something of French character, but it would be immediately recognized as having been painted by an American.

George Bellows was through and through an American. His great enthusiasm for his own country, and his ability to find an abundance of material, whether in town or in country, on the noisy docks, or in the quiet studio, in the world of sport, or in the deep silences, made him a unique figure in the modern art field. During the comparatively few years given to painting he accomplished so much in strong, masterly work that he now holds a foremost place in the annals of American art. In fact he is now regarded as one of America's greatest painters.

STUDY FOR APPRECIATION

1. What are the distinguishing characteristics of this painter's style?
2. Point out elements of his style in this picture.

   Does this add to the art quality of his work? How?
3. What gives the feeling of life and activity?

   What gives the feeling of strength, power, and stability?

   How does the artist achieve this?
4. Explain how the eye travels over the picture.

   Why does it follow this path?
5. Where is the center of interest?

   Where are secondary interests?
6. How has the artist treated the center of interest? Why?

   Explain how the pattern of light has been unified.
7. Are the colors related?

   Explain the difference in values.
8. Does the artist use chiefly color, line, or pattern of light and dark to give art form to his picture?
9. Trace the important parts of the composition which show the pattern.
10. Who is the artist?

    What is his place in the modern art world?

Related Music: MARCH ....*Hollaender*

THE VIRGIN
Freer Gallery of Art, Washington, D.C.

ARTIST: Abbot Handerson Thayer
SCHOOL: American
DATES: 1849-1921

THE VIRGIN

"Beauty is its own excuse for being." So sang the poet Keats a century ago. These words of the English poet are constantly suggested in viewing the pictures of Abbot Handerson Thayer, American painter of the ideal.

It is said that the constant aspiration of Mr. Thayer was to express his conception of ideal beauty as seen in young American womanhood and childhood. This, however, was not a mere material beauty of face and figure, but that intangible, ethereal something within, which gives expression to the lines and contours of the human face and form, the spirit. He had the rare insight and ability to suggest those subtle but essential characteristics which give meaning to the external form.

Mr. Thayer's art was not that of "real pictures of real people." He was not a realist. Likewise Mr. Thayer was not concerned with telling a story. The beauty of this master's paintings lies not in their meaning but rather in their FEELING. The aim of the artist was "not to convey meaning but FEELING."

In viewing his beautiful painting, "The Virgin" of the Freer Gallery, one is not concerned with the personalities, who they may be, or where they are going, but rather with the FEELING which the painting inspires.

Immediately the mind responds to its beauty. Why? What magic in the painter's brush has power to touch and thrill the aesthetic sense? Is it color? Is it design? Yes, it is all this plus that indefinable essence which comes from within out, and is seen in the play of feature, the line and poise of the human figure. Mr. Thayer sought to bring to the unseeing eye, by the tangible means of drawing, design, and color, that which is intangible, but which may be called spirituality.

Over the hilltop with light buoyant step come the three advancing figures. Erect and with heads up they step lightly along. Perhaps it is this buoyancy of movement that inspires the first response to the picture's beauty. Linked so closely with this, however, are the design elements of color and pattern, that no one element can be said to cause this response. Instead, all three combine to create the feeling for and recognition of beauty.

The tall central figure is the familiar type idealized in many of his paintings. The two children, one on each side, have been raised above the merely human. Their expressive faces and deep forward-looking eyes suggest the vision.   On they come, buoyant, free!

The landscape is rather vague.   The hill-top wears a dull gray-green herbage, a color which tones, in quiet harmony and loveliness, with the hues of the fluttering draperies.   In the distance, a bank of soft cloud rolls up to right and left, taking on the appearance of wings.   This, you will notice, adds much to the feeling of forward movement.   Beyond the clouds the beautiful blue of the sky becomes an admirable background for the contour and color of the lovely head.   Just above, a bit of overhanging branch, in full blossom, crosses the margin, lending a caressing note to the scene.

In many of Mr. Thayer's most famous paintings the ideal figures have been given an added ethereal quality by the great outspreading wings.   This artist, by giving wings to his figures, carries his idealization of the form still further, indicating by this that they lay no claim to realism.   Thus their message of loveliness simply unfolds to the mind of those who FEEL.

Beautiful color is a charm of all the Thayer pictures.   Note the subtle relation existing in the color of the draperies, the hilltop, and the dull gray cloud just behind. How refined is the gray of the little girl's dress against the gray-green foliage and gray cloud! How fitting the green cloth about her shoulders! Opposite, in the drapery of the little lad, is the same feeling for harmony and a refined sense of color tones. With what exquisite sense of color pattern the gray-yellow of the virgin's drapery unifies the color tones of the painting.

Combined with this charm of color is the artist's innate feeling of appropriate design or pattern. Beautiful composition, the balance of form, and play of line, distinguishes all his work.

Pyramidal arrangement is emphasized by the lines of extended arms. Interest centers about the head where these lines converge and where there is the added emphasis of cloud-forms which serve to frame in the head. Rhythmic repetition of the diagonal lines of drapery give the feeling of forward movement.

Though this famous painting is called "The Virgin", it could as well be given other appropriate names. This title, in fact,

70

expresses no particular meaning, for the picture was not conceived to teach. Its message is to please, to inspire. The success of the picture is not in its meaning, but in the FEELING conveyed.

In the expression of the human countenance Abbot Thayer is said to stand alone. It is his ability to express through physical beauty his idealized conception of spiritual quality that sets him apart as a painter of individuality and distinction.

Even in his own day, Mr. Thayer's art was recognized as enduring. The quality which he brought to his work, his supreme ability to recognize character, his innate sense of design, his instinctive feeling for color, and his great delicacy of feeling, are fundamentals.

Because of his high appreciation and understanding of these fundamentals his pictures are not restricted to any time or place. They may be enjoyed by all people everywhere. Thus his art is enduring, universal.

A prophecy, written shortly after his death in 1921, is being remarkably fulfilled. "Abbot H. Thayer, it is safe to predict, will be regarded in years to come as one of the great artists of this age."

Abbot H. Thayer is today recognized as among the greatest of American artists.

THE ARTIST.

Shining in the constellation of great American artists is the star of Abbot Handerson Thayer. His is an individuality unique, a talent distinctive. Not only artist but scientist as well, Mr. Thayer's name lives today in two distinct lines of American thought, art and science. In each he has made a valuable contribution to American development.

Born in Boston in 1849, he passed all his boyhood in rural New England. Here it was that he developed the two lines of interest which he followed all through his life. As a boy he spent much time in the open air, enjoying the woods and fields. He was captivated by nature in her every aspect. He took keen delight in the flowers, the foliage, bugs, beetles, and in all living creatures. He delighted in making exact drawings of the various specimens which he had collected. Later as a young man the coloring of these creatures, so close to nature, intensely interested him, and he began a serious but fascinating study of what is called protective coloring of animals.

We think of this in connection with the chameleon, which changes color with every change of habitat; the moth, which resembles the dried leaves among which it hangs; the caterpillar, which resembles a tiny twig; and many animals of the jungle whose protective coloring makes them unseen.

As a result of this continuous study and research Mr. Thayer's valuable book, "Concealing Coloration in the Animal Kingdom", was later published. Strange as it may seem, the theories which the artist had worked out proved to be none other than the principles of camouflage. These principles were later adopted and used by the United States and other countries in the World War. His original specimens demonstrating natural protective coloring have been carefully preserved, and today may be seen in the Natural History Museums of London, Oxford, Cambridge and other cities.

His great interest in bird life led him to make still another contribution of his time and effort in behalf of his feathered friends. In 1900, when fashion decreed the use of plumage, especially that of the gull and the birds of the Atlantic sea coast, for millinery purposes, Mr. Thayer raised a fund and initiated a movement for securing laws to prevent this traffic in their plumage. As a result a new law, known as the "Audubon Law", was passed in eleven states. This was in large measure the beginning of the educational work now being done by the National

Audubon Societies. These activities of Mr. Thayer's mature life are undoubtedly traceable to his childhood's love of nature and the great out-of-doors.

It was while the artist was still a child that his father observed his decided taste for drawing, and particularly for drawing these natural specimens of field and farm. His ready sympathy and interest stimulated the lad in his endeavors. During the years from fifteen to eighteen he found time after school hours to study with the town jeweler, who was very clever in the drawing of animals. This appealed to the young lad. He soon drew so well that he was able to sell his work. At first his dog portraits brought ten dollars; later on they brought as high as fifty dollars.

Naturally young Mr. Thayer decided that he wanted to be an animal painter. With this in mind he began, while still in his teens, his serious study at the New York School of Design. In the city of New York he soon became known as an animal painter.

By and by when he reached twenty-six he planned to continue his studies in Paris. It was in Paris that his first interest in animal painting was supplanted by an interest in portrait painting.

Upon his return to America, with other

artists who had studied in Paris, he found it difficult to adjust his foreign training to American taste. The models, the peasant, and figures in classic drapery to which they had grown accustomed in the French capital, were strangely out of place in America. Moreover by this time the camera had been so perfected and popularized that it supplied the place of the painted portrait.

Nevertheless Mr. Thayer began to paint portraits. It took both time and effort to adjust himself to the new condition. Among his earliest portraits are those of his wife and children. These portraits soon made a great impression.

Strangest of all is the fact that the field of portrait painting gradually disclosed a still greater talent and one for which he is justly famous, that of portraying the idealized conception of the human face and form.

True, these may still be portraits, for the human face with its meaning was always of great interest to the artist. The idealized portrait, however, is less individual, and more universal in its appeal.

In several of his ideal portraits an angel is the principal figure. This removes the conception still further from the realm of earth, and imparts an ethereal power and dignity to his work.

His "Winged Figure", the figure of an angel seated upon a rock above the grave of Robert Louis Stevenson, is a powerful creation. "Caritas", of the Boston Museum of Fine Arts, is filled with that dignity and spirituality which envelops all his pictures, especially those that belong to his later period. "Caritas", "The Madonna Enthroned", and "The Virgin" of the Freer Gallery, are his favorite types of composition, that is, a young woman in the center, sometimes seated, sometimes standing, and a child on each side.

Though Mr. Thayer painted many portraits, his best are those of the people nearest him, his wife and children. These same faces appear again and again in his idealized portraits. In "The Virgin" of the Freer Gallery one recognizes the beautiful face of the elder daughter, and also his two younger children.

Mr. Thayer painted few landscapes. His "Winter Sunrise on Monadnock", however, in the Metropolitan Museum of Art in New York City, is said to be one of the finest examples of American landscape ever painted.

Finally, it must be said of Abbot Thayer that his work revealed himself, a rare spirit giving to the world his ideal of beauty.

STUDY FOR APPRECIATION

1. Would you classify this picture as figure painting, portraiture, or imaginative painting?
2. Does the picture please you? Why?
   What do you feel to be the most impressive feature?
3. What distinguishes the faces?
4. What gives movement?
   Point out groups of rhythmic lines which help.
   Do the clouds help? How?
5. Does "color" add to the "feeling" of the picture?
   Are colors closely related or strongly contrasted?
6. Does the picture show design form?
   Do the clouds help?
7. What is the general form of composition?
   Trace, showing plan.
8. Who is the artist?
   What is his particular gift to American art?
9. What contribution has he made to science?
   How were these discoveries made?
10. Name several of his famous paintings.

Related Music: THE YEAR'S AT THE SPRING
Mrs. Beach
TO A WILD ROSE..........*MacDowell*

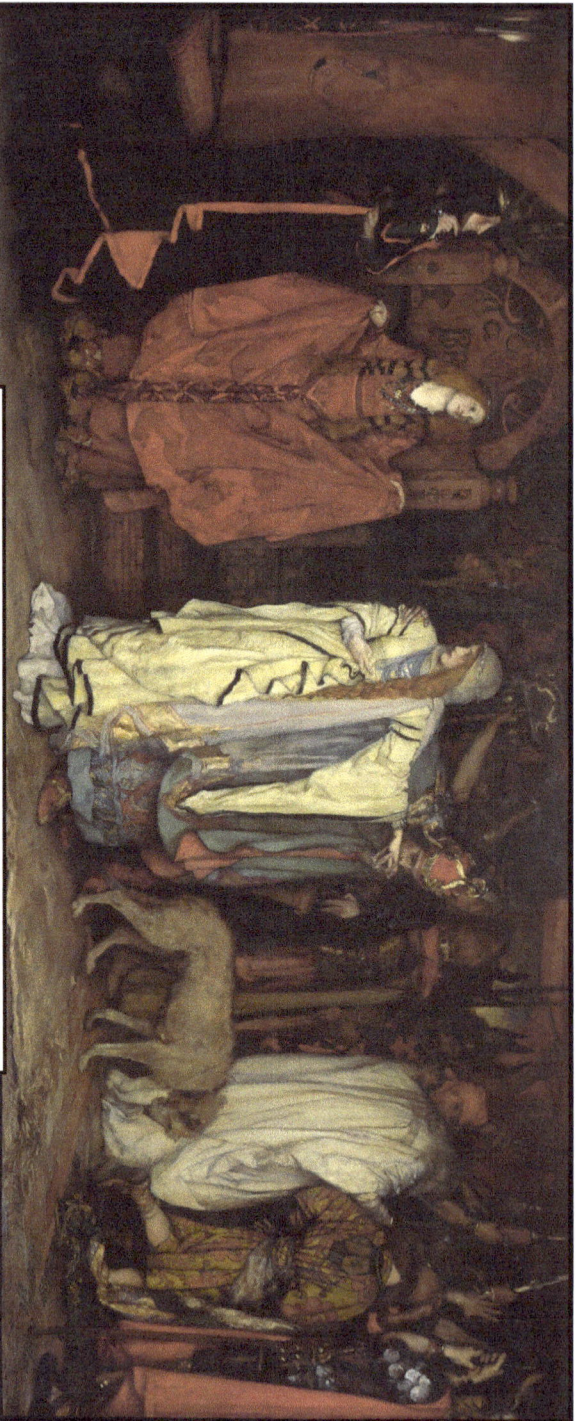

KING LEAR
Metropolitan Museum, New York

ARTIST: Edwin Austin Abbey
SCHOOL: American
DATES: 1852-1911

KING LEAR.

Among the famous literary painters in American art, Edwin Austin Abbey holds first place. His pictorial interpretation of that ancient legend, "The Holy Grail", in the Boston Public Library, and of many Shakespearian plays, has won for him great honor, and a place unique in the art world.

The story of Lear, king of Britain, and his three daughters, Goneril, Regan, and Cordelia, has been immortalized by that greatest of dramatists, William Shakespeare. Mr. Abbey has chosen the point of supreme interest in the story, and pictured it in a beautiful composition known as "King Lear", which now hangs in the Metropolitan Museum of New York City.

As the story goes, the aged king was worn out with the burdens of government. Wishing to be free from these responsibilities for the remaining years of his life, he planned to call together his daughters and learn from them which loved him best. He then intended to divide his kingdom among them in proportion to the affection which each professed.

Goneril, the eldest, declared that she loved her father more than words could tell; that he was dearer to her than life and liberty; dearer than her own eyes.

The old king was delighted. He believed the extravagant words of the cunning daughter, and bestowed upon her one third of his kingdom.

Regan, like her sister, professed her love for the king was beyond words. She declared that her greatest joy was in caring for her aged father.

Again Lear blessed himself for having two such dutiful daughters, and bestowed upon Regan one third of his kingdom. Then he turned to his youngest daughter, Cordelia, who had always been his pride and joy. Cordelia, however, knew that her sisters' words of endearment were only cunning expressions devised to wheedle the old king out of his dominions. So while her father awaited her reply, she answered simply that she loved and honored him according to her duty, neither more nor less.

The king was shocked. Excited and blinded by disappointment and anger, he was unable to distinguish between flattery and sincerity. While in this temper, he divided the remaining third of his kingdom between Goneril and Regan, investing them and their husbands with all power, revenue, and the execution of the laws.

Astonished and alarmed, the attendants looked on at this hasty action of the king.

The suitors for Cordelia's hand, the Duke of Burgundy and the King of France, were called in to hear the king's decision. All present doubted that either of the suitors would accept Cordelia, now that she had no fortune. As expected, the Duke of Burgundy declined the match. The King of France, however, knowing the sincerity of Cordelia and the craftiness of her sisters, took her hand, saying that her virtues were a dowry above a kingdom. He bade her take farewell of her sisters and go with him to be Queen of France. The grief-stricken king turned, and with his attendants prepared to leave the hall.

The rich colorings, the costumes and settings of such a scene, appealed to the artistic imagination of Mr. Abbey. He pictures the court scene with Cordelia the central figure. To her right stand her sisters, to her left the departing king and attendants.

How easily our interest centers upon Cordelia. She has just spoken burning words of reproof to her sisters. She stands with eyes reproachfully fastened upon them, while the King of France bends to kiss her hand. Our eyes naturally follow the gaze of Cordelia, passing to Goneril and Regan, and then back again to Cordelia. In this way the artist threads his way from figure to figure, drawing the three into a group. Again, Cordelia's outstretched arm leads the way to the bowed figure of the departing king, then back again to the central figure. Thus the whole picture-plan is related in every part, and becomes a unit centering about Cordelia.

By leading lines in the composition the eye is carried to right and left of the center. Following these leads, the eye traverses the entire picture and returns again to the "center of interest."

To emphasize and beautify his picture-pattern, the artist has used certain colors, and distributed them over the composition where they are best fitted to give interest and balance to the design. As the "center of interest" he makes Cordelia most prominent by her place in the picture, and further gives emphasis by painting her costume in the lightest hues. Tints of light blue and delicate green drape her figure. A repetition of this light note, more gray, however, in the robe of King Lear, draws our attention over to this group at the left.

Opposite stands the sinister figure of Goneril. As if the artist were using color and form to depict her crafty character, he clothes her in black and red. Her pose as well as the color suggests her disdain and scorn. There she stands, erect, swathed in black, her sharply outlined features propped upon a likewise sharply outlined hand. This straight vertical accent of face, hand, arm, and red edge of the robe, strikingly emphasize the force of her contemptuous attitude.

The figure of Regan is triumphant as she lifts and spreads her rich red robe. These same reds are repeated opposite in the mantle of the standing soldier, and again, toned off, in the robes of the king's attendants.

How depressed is the group as it leaves the hall! Could a figure be more expressive of crushed hope than that of the bowed king, feebly departing from the scene!

As the central figure in the dramatic scene stands Cordelia, greatest of all in her love for the aged king.

What a beautiful figure she is! She wears the characteristic costume of the twelfth century, long flowing robe, enveloping mantle, and filmy headdress. The women of that distant day permitted their hair to grow to great length, and arranged it in two braids, intertwining it with ribbon and flowers. True to her Saxon type Cordelia is pictured with flaxen hair. See how the long braid falls in with the line of the blue veil; see how the hanging sleeve repeats this line, giving a statuesque beauty to the figure.

Sometimes the head was covered with a short head-dress, and the throat swathed in a wimple, as the artist has pictured Goneril.

Notice the low rich color of the background. There is the massive chair and the stacked weapons reminiscent of medieval days. All this detail, however, is well nigh lost as it melts into the grayed-reds, greens, and browns of the background. Against this rich color the five figures of Cordelia, Goneril, Regan, King Lear, and the King of France stand forth in the order of their importance in the story, while the harmonious background serves to hold the group in one masterful composition.

Thus the artist has told his story, not in words, to be sure. He has, however, through his understanding of color and design-form, pictured the disappointed king, the crafty daughters, the lovely Cordelia, quite as clearly as the great Shakespeare has interpreted these characters in words. Beside the literary art of Shakespeare we may place the pictorial art of Edwin Austin Abbey, and there find recorded the same story, in glowing color and superb design.

THE ARTIST

Edwin Austin Abbey has been called "the painter of the past." His absorbing interest in the people and times of long ago, and his masterly interpretation of these age-old stories have earned for him this distinction.

Like many others in the art world, Mr. Abbey rose to eminence through his own effort and determination. His boyhood was spent in the quiet city of Philadelphia, just before the Civil War. As a lad in school he showed a decided liking for only one thing, and that was drawing. His parents, however, gave no particular attention to the lad's native ability. They had other plans. Only the ministry, medicine, or law seemed worthy fields for their son. Young Abbey's distaste, however, for the professions settled the matter. He decided to learn a trade. Accordingly he was apprenticed to a Philadelphia publisher. Here he would learn to set type and in time become a good printer.

While working at the printing trade he found time to attend the drawing classes of the Philadelphia Academy of Fine Arts, and spent his evenings working industriously at his sketches.

His employer soon discovered that the boy was not at heart a printer. At the same time he observed his ability in drawing. One day he looked over his sketches, and frankly told the lad that they were worthy of the best magazine in the country. Accordingly he sent him with a letter of introduction to Harper's Weekly. The young lad was thrilled! Harper's Weekly was just now making a record for itself by its war-time illustrations. Among the artists at the front who were supplying sketches for the paper was Winslow Homer, destined to be America's greatest marine painter.

Young Abbey's sketches pleased the head of the Art Department, and he was engaged at seven dollars a week. Abbey felt that his dream was coming true! His first drawing appeared in 1871, and from that time he met with increasing success.

Eight years later came his first great commission. He was invited to illustrate the poems of Robert Herrick. This necessitated first hand study and a visit to England. This visit proved to be a farewell to America, for he was so pleased with rural England that he decided to make that country his home. His illustrations of literary subjects, especially those from Shakespeare, rapidly brought him before the public eye.

Soon came the commission for the Boston mural decoration, "The Quest of the Holy Grail." Three American artists, Mr. Whistler

Mr. Sargent, and Mr. Abbey, were invited to decorate all but the main hallway, which was given to the French painter, Puvis de Chavannes. Mr. Whistler declined, but Mr. Sargent and Mr. Abbey, both living in England, worked side by side in the spacious studio on Mr. Abbey's estate, developing their decorations for these large wall spaces.

When certain sections of Mr. Abbey's "Sir Galahad" series were completed, they were exhibited in London before being sent to America. They made a profound impression.

Following this wider recognition of his work, Mr. Abbey was invited to paint the coronation scene of Edward VII. Many were the annoyances of the painter with this vast work. Such a scene necessitated the painting of many portraits. The tardiness of the sitters in meeting their appointments at the studio, and their general thoughtlessness greatly annoyed the artist. He is said to have remarked on more than one occasion, that the king and queen were the only members of the group who met their appointments promptly, and were pleasant and considerate. His experience in this work led him to decline a later invitation extended by George V to paint the scene of his coronation. "The Coronation Scene of Edward VII" now hangs in Buckingham Palace.

Foreign scenes and settings held a peculiar fascination for the artist. Costumes and accoutrements of the middle ages as well as those of later centuries captivated him. It is said that he consumed books on the subject with feverish interest, would go miles on an archeological venture, and was willing to make any effort to add to his historical knowledge.

In looking back over the work of Mr. Abbey, it seems that all he had previously done, his pen and ink illustrations, his work in oils and water colors, and his fund of historical knowledge, only fitted him for his last great work, and that in his own state,—the murals of the Pennsylvania capitol at Harrisburg. Here upon the walls of the capitol building he has left a series of historical pictures commemorating the making of that great commonwealth. Here one reads in picture of the statesmanship of William Penn, Benjamin Franklin, and Robert Morris. It is indeed a memorial to Pennsylvania's famous men, and a record of their achievements. Thus, as always, it is Mr. Abbey's talent for historical themes, whether age-old legends or history in the making, that distinguishes his work.

Decorated by foreign governments and receiving all possible honors at home, Edwin Austin Abbey achieved the distinction of a unique leadership among American artists.

STUDY FOR APPRECIATION

1. What is the distinguishing character of Mr. Abbey's art?
2. Name the several characters in the painting in the order of their importance.

   How does this compare with their prominence in the story?

   Does this give merit to the painting? How?
3. How has Cordelia been made the center of interest?

   How has the artist unified his pattern?

   Does the dog add to the design? How?
4. Would you say that the artist has used chiefly color, or line, or dark and light pattern to secure unity?

   Would you say he used all three?
5. Does the artist show choices of color in telling his story? Explain.

   Does this help interpret the picture? How?

   Does the pose of the figures help? How?
6. Which do you think the most impressive figure? Why?
7. Why has detail in the background been eliminated?

   Does this add to the design? How?
8. Name one other famous work by Mr. Abbey drawn from literary sources.

Related Music: SYMPHONY IN B MINOR (unfinished) ....*Schubert*
ADAGIO LAMENTASO............
Tschaikowsky

BATTERSEA BRIDGE
National Gallery, London

ARTIST: James McNeil Whistler
SCHOOL: American
DATES: 1834-1903

NOCTURNE IN BLUE AND SILVER
Battersea Bridge.

Ever loyal to his own peculiar theories as to just what a picture should be, Mr. Whistler called this, his celebrated painting of the old Battersea Bridge, a "Nocturne in Blue and Silver."

True, Battersea Bridge which spans the Thames at Chelsea was the inspiration for the picture, but the poetic vision of the artist transformed mere masonry, lost in an evening's haze, into something far more lovely than a material bridge. To the casual passerby the old bridge, high above the embankment, meant nothing more than an easy transit from one side to the other. To Mr. Whistler, however, seen from below with its great mass cutting the night sky, it became not a bridge but a harmony of form and color, like a nocturne in blue and silver.

Mr. Whistler often declared that it is not the person or thing painted that is of consequence, but always the WAY it is painted. He insisted that "as music is the poetry of sound so painting is the poetry of sight." This was ever uppermost in his mind. His whole aim in painting seemed to be the arrangement and combination of color into beautiful harmonies as pleasing to the eye as is music to the ear. To make his theories still more clear he gave his pictures such names as, "An Arrangement in Gray and Black," "Symphony in White," "Nocturne in Blue and Gold." Thus you see he was always emphasizing the color, color harmony, and color arrangement.

In outdoor painting it was the twilight hour that held the greatest charm for the artist. Then, he says, "the evening mists clothe the riverside with poetry as with a veil, and the poor buildings lose themselves in the sky, and the tall chimneys become campanili, and the warehouses are palaces in the night, and the whole city hangs in the heavens, and fairyland is before us."

Such, indeed, must have been his vision of old Battersea Bridge, as the evening shadows enfolded it.

See the solid form of the bridge as under a veil, outlined against the hazy sky! See the beautiful spacing of the canvas! In so pleasing a way has the upright pier been placed that it could be moved neither to the right nor left without marring the beauty of the spacing. The swing of the bridge above and the line of the bank below complete this perfect arrangement of picture space.

Under the veil of night the sky is softly silvered. The water, too, takes on the same misty light, while the "poor buildings" and "tall chimneys" are merged into a dark, indistinct mass.　In the fore-front where the water becomes a deep grayed-blue, the dark barge and the silhouetted figure add a strong note compelling the interest to keep within the picture-space.　Through this veil of silver-blue one sees the bright lights of a rocket.　Like fireflies of the night they come floating in their

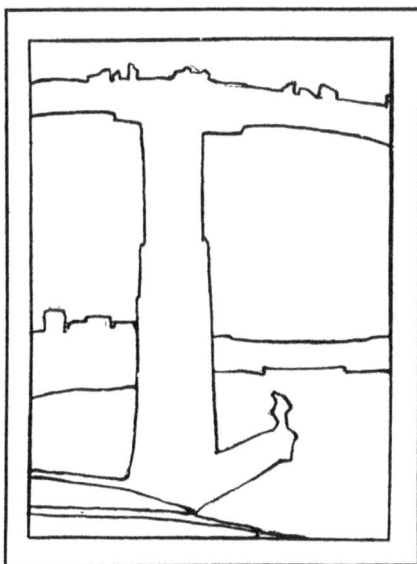

Pattern reduced to simple lines showing the s u b t l e spacing of the canvas.

downward course to the world below.　All along the opposite bank the orange lights glisten from distant windows, sending their ribbon-like reflections into the still, limpid stream.

Nearer, the bright light of the barge glows, while the barge itself, its silent figure, and the massive bridge are held in the mysterious, enveloping light of night.

To him who has eyes to see, this interpretation of the old bridge becomes, in color, tone, and arrangement, the music of the night, a "Nocturne in Blue and Silver."

In keeping with the sentiment of the painting, the color is smooth and apparently flat; not a brush stroke is visible. In both smoothness of color and beauty of composition this famous picture speaks silently of the great influence of the famous Japanese painter, Hokusai, who died about the middle of the nineteenth century. Mr. Whistler was most generous in his praise of the famous oriental, and frequently spoke of the great contribution he had made to his own understanding of art. In fact it was only to Hokusai, the Japanese, and Velasquez, the Spaniard, that Mr. Whistler paid highest tribute. No two artists influenced him more. On one occasion it is said that the artist drew himself up, in the superior manner which was so characteristic, and said: "Yes, there is Velasquez, Hokusai, and myself."

Though today no artists are following Mr. Whistler's style, nevertheless his art is established. Said John Alexander, "No more active influence than that of Mr. Whistler's has impressed itself upon American life."

THE ARTIST.

James A. McNeill Whistler, considered by many the greatest of American artists, was a man of decided individuality, in his thinking, his speech, his personality, and in everything with which he had to do. He could never be judged by ordinary standards, for he was a law unto himself. Consequently he was a man of many enemies and few close friends.

One of his peculiar traits was his dislike for all references to time. He never carried a watch, and would not tolerate the tick of a clock in his studio. He had a peculiar dislike for dates and places when they registered time in his own life. The story is told of a little child who innocently inquired of the artist where he was born.

"I never was born, my child," was the reply; "I came from above."

The place of the artist's birth, however, is now known to have been Lowell, Massachusetts, and the year 1834. This was only incidentally discovered in later years. In his mother's diary under date of July 10, 1844, she tells of a poem that "Jamie" put under her plate at breakfast, as a surprise on his tenth birthday. Thus it was that the distasteful date was revealed.

Whistler came of a long line of fighters. His grandfather, Major John Whistler, ran away from home and joined the British under Burgoyne. At the close of the war he entered the American army. In 1803 he was sent west to construct Fort Dearborn, as a frontier defence against the Indians. This little fort proved to be the nucleus of the present great city of Chicago.

Whistler's father was known as Major George Washington Whistler, of the United States Army. At West Point he won distinction as an engineer, and his reputation was such that he was commissioned to build important railroads in this country. Later, when the boy James was about eight years old, Major Whistler was sent to Russia to superintend the building of the railway between Moscow and St. Petersburg.

After nine years in Russia, and following Major Whistler's death, the family returned to America. The lad "Jamie" was then a youth of seventeen.

Then it was that the mother began to plan a military career for her son. Like his forebears, she wished him to gain distinction in the army. The youth, encouraged by his mother and urged on by a soldierly uncle, also favored this course. Accordingly after a short time young Whistler was admitted to West Point.

While he was a soldier at heart and by

heritage, his nature rebelled at the discipline of the Academy. He was seldom on time for his classes, many times absent, and finally at the end of three years was dismissed. Though he failed in most of his studies, he led his class in drawing.

It was after his dismissal from West Point that his art career began in earnest. At twenty-one he went to Europe, and never returned to America. After visiting England he went to Paris. Here he met with many failures. Instead of discouraging him, such lack of appreciation of his art only aroused his indignation and disgust.

It was while living in Paris, just before leaving to make his home in England, that a new influence came into his life. He became fascinated by the wares of a little Japanese shop. Here he saw porcelains, embroideries, lacquers, and beautiful Japanese prints. The composition and flat tone of color in this art of the East remained with him always. Today it is the distinguishing characteristic of his work.

Mr. Whistler's art was so different from what people had known that at first they did not understand it. As an example of this lack of understanding, one incident will suffice to tell the whole story.

In 1873 Mr. Whistler submitted for exhibition the well-known portrait of his mother under the name, "An Arrangement in Gray and Black." The jurors refused to accept it, until one of their number indignantly threatened to resign as he exclaimed: "It shall never be said of me that I served on a committee that refused such a work as that!" Today this painting is accounted one of the masterpieces of the world.

Though we usually think of Mr. Whistler as a painter, he was equally famed as an etcher. In fact in this art he is regarded as second only to the great Dutch master, Rembrandt van Rijn.

Among his many masterpieces the portrait of his mother, "An Arrangement in Gray and Black", is probably best known. This picture was purchased by the French government in 1891, and placed in the Luxembourg. In 1926 it was removed to the Louvre. This is the first picture by an American artist to be given this distinctive honor.

Another of Mr. Whistler's great portraits is that of Thomas Carlyle. This was purchased by the city of Glasgow, Scotland, and now hangs in the city museum.

Though these two portraits with a few other famous pictures are in foreign galleries, and a few characteristic paintings are scattered here and there in America, it is in the Freer

Gallery, Washington, D. C., that a Whistler collection has been made. Here one may study the varied aspects of the master's art.

In this collection are several "Nocturnes," a collection of water colors, pastels, and etchings, "The Music Room," "The Balcony," and the famous "Peacock Room."

The episode of the Peacock Room is one which throws much light on the amazing independence of the artist. This now historical room was at one time the dining room in the home of Mr. Frederick Leyland, a friend of Mr. Whistler. Mr. Leyland had purchased one of Mr. Whistler's pictures, "A Princess from the Land of Porcelain," and hung it in his dining room, the walls of which were covered with embossed leather. One day the artist, calling at the Leyland home, found that the embossed leather walls were sadly out of harmony with his painting. He begged permission to bring the room into harmony with his picture. It was agreed. Mr. Whistler consented to do the work while Mr. Leyland was absent from home. The artist set to work with his usual enthusiasm, and quite forgetful of limitations, he kept on until he had covered the walls of the entire room with a decoration in which peacocks and their feathers were the motive of design.

When Mr. Leyland returned he found, much

to his surprise, that his dining room had been transformed. Further he did not agree with the artist as to the artistic merit of the decoration. This of course disgusted the artist, and to show his feeling he caricatured the situation by painting two peacocks, one in the guise of patron, the other as artist; the one guarding a pile of stones which the other insisted belonged to him. Naturally the owner protested this abuse of his home. On the other hand Mr. Whistler insisted that he was right. "You should be grateful to me," he said; "I have made you famous. My work will live when you are forgotten. Still, perchance in the dim ages to come you may be remembered as the proprietor of the 'Peacock Room.'"

With striking accuracy this prophecy has been fulfilled. Mr. Leyland's wealth is scattered and he would be well-nigh forgotten were it not for the famous "Peacock Room." This room, which has since been moved from the Leyland home to the Freer Gallery, has been pronounced "the most perfect mural decoration of modern times."

Though the misunderstanding of Mr. Whistler's art by the public of his day was due to his very original theories regarding artistic expression, today, in the art history of the world, James A. McNeill Whistler is accounted a master.

STUDY OF APPRECIATION

1. What were the artist's theories about picture making?
2. How did the artist see this picture of the old bridge?
3. Does the color help to interpret the meaning of the picture?
   Are colors related?
   How many values do you find?
4. Does the picture show design form?
   Point out the fine space relations.
   Make a sketch showing composition.
5. Why are the rockets and lights introduced?
   What keeps the interest within the picture?
6. Does the artist use color, line, or dark and light pattern to secure unity?
   Would you say he used all three art elements?
7. Who is the artist?
   What two artists influenced him most?
8. What is his greatest portrait?
   Where does it hang?
   What are its distinguishing characteristics?
9. Name other famous works.

Related Music: NOCTURNE IN G MAJOR..*Chopin*
JEWELS OF THE MADONNA
—Intermezzo ....*Wolf-Ferrari*

THE APOTHEOSIS OF PITTSBURGH
Carnegie Institute, Pittsburgh

ARTIST: John White Alexander
SCHOOL: American
DATES: 1856-1915

THE APOTHEOSIS OF PITTSBURGH

The Crowning of Labor
From the murals of Carnegie Institute
John W. Alexander.

When John W. Alexander was commissioned to decorate the walls of Carnegie Institute, Pittsburgh, he departed in both subject and style from all previous forms of mural decoration. Never before had the subject of "Labor" been considered a worthy theme for the decoration of a public building. Yet "The Crowning of Labor" was chosen by this eminent painter as a most fitting subject for the walls of this great institution.

Pittsburgh, the Steel City of the east, is a Center of Industry. Day and night her machinery thunders. Her seething furnaces continually pour forth a lurid glare. Her tall chimneys are lost in clouds of rolling smoke. It is here that the sinewy forms of half-clad iron-workers, immersed in clouds of steam, bend and reach and sway. Here the toil of the workers becomes the foundation upon which the institutions of a people are builded. Such is the city that Labor has made great!

The contribution that Labor has made to the greatness of Pittsburgh furnished the inspiration for this magnificent tribute, "The Apotheosis of Pittsburgh."

These famous murals occupy large paneled spaces, in three stories, around the four walls of the "open well" or entrance hall of the building. This hall is approximately sixty-six feet square. A massive staircase rises from the center of the first floor, and turning to right and left leads to a gallery about the second story. This in turn communicates by staircase with the third story in such a way that the great "open well" is unobstructed.

As a central figure about which the artist has woven his story of Labor's triumph is the city of Pittsburgh, personified as a knight in steel armor. The knightly figure, about to be crowned, occupies the most conspicuous panel of the second story series. All other panels in the vast mural scheme, both those on the first floor and those on the third, lead to and emphasize this inspiring center of decoration.

About the first floor are the labor murals, fifteen in all. Here are the workers, their heroic forms partly visible through clouds of smoke and vapor. The rising clouds and the illumination from flaming furnaces carry up, pattern-like, to the panels of the second story. Here, with the mail-clad figure of Pittsburgh as a center, is pictured, not the activity of labor, but Labor's triumph.

Above in the third story are the people, the populace—men, women and children of vigorous, happy, sturdy mien—joining in the great triumphal procession.

The spirit and movement of all the panels of this vast allegory combine as one, centering in the triumphant figure of Pittsburgh.

In this panel a dark, jagged cloud bursts into the picture from below. Immediately above, relieved against a mass of dark, is poised the prophetic figure of the knight. Just why the artist chose to symbolize the city as a knight in armor is left to the imagination. Though clad in complete coat of mail there is no suggestion of the militant knight of the middle ages. He seems rather a vision, a prophecy taking form out of the clouds of mist and vapor that hang over the city. As the figure materializes still more to our vision, one notes that the sword is lowered, removing the conception still further from that of the militant knight. Note how the sword, tipping the dark cloud, pulls the pattern of the panel together, and adds as well to the dignity of the knightly figure.

To the left only three of the heralding figures are seen. With trumpets raised to their lips they proclaim to all the world the triumph of industry in this, the great steel center. The mass of dark cloud beneath their feet floats off to the left in a rolling bank of dull color, supporting in the adjoining panels the remaining figures. These grow more and more delicate and shadowy as they gradually disappear in the distance.

To the right is a series of great white-winged figures which come like huge birds winging their way through space, bringing forward their gifts as a tribute to the city. The first of these to reach the knight pauses, then raises the golden wreath, the crown of the city's triumph. Thus is the dream of Pittsburgh's greatness about to be consummated! Thus is the triumph of Labor immortalized!

Though the figures to the immediate right and left of the knight are continuous with those of adjoining panels, the interest here, by sheer force of composition, is turned within the panel itself. Though the trumpets of the heralding angels are raised to the outside world, the extended arm of the nearest figure leads the eye unconsciously to the knight in armor. Again, the action of the great white-winged figure, with arms upraised above the knight's head, centers the attention here. And still again the jagged cloud, catching the eye, leads along the glittering line of the sword to the steel clad figure.

Color also plays an important part in centering the attention within the panel. The dark elongated cloud with the glimmering coat of mail relieved against it is in startling contrast to the lighter and more delicate tones of the composition.   In fact color, line, and pattern of dark and light, all three, have a part in the artistic development of the composition of the panel.

A simple line rendering, showing pattern and the way in which lines of the composition sustain the "center of interest."

Throughout the vast decoration one is impressed by the way in which the great wall pictures are harmonized with the architectural design.   They seem to grow naturally out of the architecture, and at the same time complete it. All through the painting the grayish marble of the wall and frames of the panels has been kept in mind. Again and again it is reflected in effect in the grayish yellow tones of the painting. Thus the two, the painting and architecture, are brought together and become a composite whole.

Time was when decorations were placed upon walls without any thought of adapting their design to the architectural form of the interior, or was harmony of color considered.

It is to the great Italian painters of the fifteenth century, and to that modern French master, Puvis de Chavannes, that we of today are particularly indebted for our understanding of mural decoration. Chavannes insisted, so that all the world might hear, that a WALL MUST REMAIN A WALL, that it must retain its structural nature in the building of which it is a part. This was the new idea which the French master gave to the world, and today the world recognizes that he was right.

As a wall decoration "The Apotheosis of Pittsburgh" sets a new mark in mural painting. The subject, a tribute to Labor culminating in the crowning of Pittsburgh, is an idea thoroughly American, an idea growing out of our own times and conditions. It suggests the rights and possibilities of Labor as the cornerstone of a great democracy.

In execution the work is far removed from the usual form of mural painting. When one understands something of the way in which the artist worked, his peculiar spontaneity of expression is better understood. It is said that Mr. Alexander never worked out his plan for a picture definitely before beginning in color. Instead he took his seat some little distance before his easel, and with a piece of charcoal attached to a long rod, he waited in quiet composure. Sometimes he waited an hour, sometimes longer. Then, as the thought came, he made a stroke upon the canvas, placing a figure or perhaps a dominant line of the composition. From this another would suggest itself, then another, and another. By and by with the composition in this fragmentary form, the charcoal was laid aside and the work begun in color. In this way, largely through feeling, he gradually created that which his sensitive imagination had pictured.

This sensitiveness of feeling for beauty in form, line, and color, and freedom in its execution is the great contributing charm to this decoration. "The Apotheosis of Pittsburgh" is far removed in conception from all other wall decorations. It is not only modern in both conception and execution, but as well a distinctly new contribution to the field of American mural decoration.

THE ARTIST.

It is a far cry from the slender youth who one day, in his early teens, ventured to interview a New York publisher offering suggestions for the improvement of penny valentines, to John White Alexander, eminent artist and foremost mural painter.

Some say "Fate," others "Luck," but in this instance it was neither. Instead of the mere chance which these words suggest, it was open-mindedness, determination, and intelligently directed endeavor which placed the laurel upon the brow of John W. Alexander.

Many stories are told of the various ways in which Mr. Alexander, when a struggling artist, tried to get on. None, however, displays his characteristic grit and pluck as does the valentine story. It is said that when the interview with the publisher failed, young Alexander was turned away with the suggestion, a mere matter of courtesy, that he might call again. He did call again. This time he was offered, half in jest, a place as office boy. To the surprise of those concerned he accepted the place. This was the beginning of his upward course.

Here he came in contact with the leading painters and illustrators of the day. This association was a source of constant inspiration to the ambitious youth. By and by it became possible for him to attend art school, and later, at the age of twenty-one, to go abroad for study.

It was while studying in Munich in 1877, that he became a student of Frank Duveneck, the distinguished American teacher who was living in that city. He joined the group known as the "Duveneck boys," who with their teacher traveled about Italy, painting as they journeyed.

When Mr. Alexander returned to America in 1881 he first gained distinction as a portrait painter. Among the notables whom he painted at this time are Oliver Wendell Holmes, John Burroughs, and Walt Whitman. Whitman's portrait is today considered one of the great portraits in the Metropolitan Museum of Art.

Later he turned to ideal figures. Having been trained to illustrate some ideal in his work, he now made these ideal figures a center for his creative imagination. Among them the best known are, "Isabella and the Pot of Basil," in the Boston Museum of Fine Arts; "A Ray of Sunlight," in the Art Institute, Chicago; and "A Study in Black and Green," in the Metropolitan Museum, New York City. In these pictures the poetic temperament of the artist is unconsciously expressed in lines and forms of rhythmic grace and beauty.

In looking back over the artistic career of

Mr. Alexander, it seems that all he had accomplished was merely a preliminary training for his later success, that of a mural painter.

In 1895 his first mural, "The Evolution of the Book," a decoration in the Library of Congress, attracted widespread attention. Later when the decorations for the new Carnegie Institute were being considered, the name of John W. Alexander was foremost.

It is said that the artist's long record both in this country and Europe was examined in every particular. His many medals, his long list of honors, his works in private and public galleries, were all duly considered. It was on the merit of his work, and that alone, that one of the most important commissions ever given to an artist in this country was awarded John W. Alexander.

Honored thus by his native city, the painter sought a theme commemorating not only the local history of Pittsburgh but also carrying with it a world-wide meaning. Thus he has spread upon the walls of this great institution a monumental allegory, picturing in color and pattern all that Pittsburgh represents in the annals of mankind, and more, the part that Labor has contributed to these achievements.

The murals of Carnegie Institute remain a worthy tribute to the great industrial city and a lasting memorial to a native son.

STUDY FOR APPRECIATION.

1. Why is this mural termed an "Allegory"?
2. Explain the artist's idea.
   In the central panel how has he translated his idea into picture?
3. Do you feel any pictorial force in the jagged cloud? What?
   Of what pictorial value is the dark cloud behind the knight?
   Would you like the design better if the sword were raised?
   In what position does it contribute most design value?
4. How is the attention carried from the heralding figures on the left to the knight?
   From the white-winged figure?
   What quality does this give to the design?
5. Would you say that the artist has used chiefly color, or line, or dark and light pattern, to secure unity?
   Would you say he had used all three?
6. Name two reasons for this mural being considered distinctly "modern."
7. What is an essential quality of a mural painting?
   Who gave this idea to the world?
8. Who is the artist?
9. What is his distinguishing contribution to the art field?

Related Music: CORONATION MARCH..........
Kretschmer

ABRAHAM LINCOLN
Lincoln Park, Chicago

ARTIST: Augustus Saint Gaudens
SCHOOL: American
DATES: 1848-1907

ABRAHAM LINCOLN.

"O Captain! My Captain! Rise up and hear the bells;
Rise up—for you the flag is flung—for you the
bugle trills,
For you bouquets and ribboned wreaths—for you
the shores a-crowding,
For you they call, the swaying mass, their eager
faces turning."

—Walt Whitman.

There are many great portrait statues in the world. Not one, however, surpasses that impressive figure standing among the trees of Lincoln Park, Chicago. This figure of Abraham Lincoln is not only a truthful representation of the man, but more, it is a masterpiece of art. The sculptor not only pictures Lincoln, but he pictures all that Lincoln was, all that Lincoln is. In other words he has chosen to express through the medium of bronze the character of this man, his true self. Only a great artist can do this.

Lincoln stands erect, with head bowed in thought. His left hand grips the lapel of his coat, the right is held behind his back. Nothing more.

Is it possible that in this lone figure the sculptor has told of Lincoln's moral strength, his kindliness, his courage, his unswerving sense of right? Does he say through bronze, "Here stands the greatest American of them all!"

115

There are many statutes of Lincoln, all of them depicting true characteristics of the man as we know him. In this, however, the whole man, all his great qualities combined, are molded into enduring bronze.

Suppose the figure were pictured seated in the chair of state. Would this suggest strength as does the standing figure? Suppose his head were raised. Would this change the feeling? Suppose he were speaking? Would this be as impressive?

We may be sure that the sculptor's choice of pose expressed for him the great qualities of mind and heart which characterized Lincoln.

There he stands. See the long straight edges of the coat. Again, this line is repeated in the clear-cut edge of the trousers from knee to foot. Observe the line of the arm from shoulder to elbow, and the back line of the coat as well. Here are lines unbroken in their vertical strength. The artist felt the strength of clear-cut vertical lines, and he emphasizes them in this statue. He could not do this were the figure seated. In fact, all the lines would then be broken. These unbroken vertical lines give to the statue a strength which is immediately felt. They suggest the moral strength of the man.

His head is bowed. In the inclined head we

read thought, kindliness, humility, but a humility in which there is strength. The fingers of the left hand grip the lapel of the coat. This, with the advanced left foot, suggests the man of action. Strange that the figure neither moves nor observes, yet its presence thrills!

Finally we note the chair of state. We are impressed by its massive lines and enduring build. These qualities expressed in the chair are in close keeping with the character-thought of the whole work. Notice how the strong vertical edges of the chair repeat the lines of the standing figure. Thus you see, the artist keeps in mind the unity of his group. He reinforces all that he has said of Lincoln by showing something of the same qualities in the chair which is a detail of the group. Even in the lesser details of design he keeps in mind this same unity, for upon the back of the chair in low relief is carved the American eagle, carrying the olive branch of peace and the words "E PLURIBUS UNUM." By this treatment the group becomes a unit, harmonizing in every detail.

As we pause to contemplate this figure, the imagination slowly weaves a background. We see the cabin in the Kentucky woods, the lonely studies, the rail-splitter, the young lawyer. As the picture grows, the color

changes.　The blacks and reds of war shroud
the thought.　Soon these pass.　The noblest
document in history unrolls, THE EMANCI-
PATION PROCLAMATION.　Then lingers

The predominance of accented verticals gives a quality which helps to interpret the character.

the last great impression—"The Preserver of
the Nation," " the President of the Republic,"
Abraham Lincoln.

This statue of Lincoln is recognized as one
of the noblest conceptions of the great American.　It stands eleven feet six inches high.

The pedestal supporting it stands in the center of an elliptical platform some sixty by thirty feet, and six steps high. This provides a most impressive setting for the simple figure which has been characterized as "The Glorification of the Common Man, The Apotheosis of Democracy."

This impressive statue of Lincoln was unveiled in Lincoln Park, Chicago, in 1877. Though there are other distinguished statues of this great American character, Saint Gaudens' conception has frequently been quoted as the "supreme portrait" of the man.

In 1920 a replica of the statue was presented to the people of Great Britain as a gift commemorating one hundred years of friendship. The figure has been placed in a beautiful setting opposite Westminster Abbey.

THE ARTIST.

Augustus Saint Gaudens has been named the "greatest of American sculptors." It was at the Boston wharf in 1848 that a babe of six months was carried ashore by his pretty Irish mother. A courageous father had brought his little family all the way from Dublin to seek his fortune in America. Six months old, landing on American soil with an unknown future before him, such was the beginning of a life now written large in the pages of American art history. Though of French-Irish birth, Saint Gaudens is the product of American life, American education, and American ideals. For this reason America claims him as her native son.

Like other newly arrived immigrants the father found work sometimes in Boston, sometimes in New York. The child grew up under all the varied influences which only Boston and New York can give. In his own writings Saint Gaudens tells of his childhood life in the Bowery, where he says that "the smell of cake in the bakery at the corner of the street, and the stewed peaches of the German family in the same house" followed him through life.

It was after the lad had entered school that he first showed signs of talent. These signs took the form of drawings scrawled upon his slate when the teacher's back was turned, and sketches in charcoal covering walls and fences. The father watched these signs with great interest. As the boy grew older he planned on securing work for him on Saturdays and during vacations, and looked about for something of an artistic nature.

"What would you like to do?" he asked the lad of thirteen.

"I should like it if I could find something that would help me to become an artist," replied the boy.

A little later he was apprenticed to a cameo cutter. He worked at this for a number of years, cutting both shell and stone cameos. All this time, however, he was yearning for more knowledge, and specially for knowledge of drawing. Later he gained admission to Cooper Union. He was delighted. Every evening after the day's work he hurried to the school. By and by he entered the National Academy of Design. Then came Paris; then Italy.

When about twenty-six years of age he returned to America. Here he received the commission for his first work, the statue of Admiral Farragut, which was unveiled in New York in 1881. This brought him fame. Our little cameo cutter had become the leader of American sculptors!

Commissions now came fast. Among the most famous of these is the Boston monument to Colonel Robert Gould Shaw, known as the Shaw memorial. Colonel Shaw led the first regiment of colored troops organized in Massachusetts. This memorial was erected in Boston, opposite the State House, on the very spot from which Colonel Shaw's regiment left for the front in 1863.

Following this came his great work, the Lincoln, in Lincoln Park, Chicago. It was during his student days in New York that Saint

Gaudens first saw Abraham Lincoln. Before the election of Lincoln he was greatly impressed by the campaign processions, especially those showing rail fences hoisted upon carts and bearing the signs, HONEST ABE, THE RAILSPLITTER. Later he tells of looking out of the window of his studio, and there, far below in the city streets, he saw a "tall, and very dark man, bowing to the crowds on each side." This was Lincoln on his way to Washington. Later, after his asassination, he tells of his visit to Washington, and how he stood in line, a line interminable, leading to the bier of the martyred president. "Again," he says, "I went back to the end of the line to look at him again. This completed my vision of the big man." Today Saint Gaudens' name is inseparably linked with that of Abraham Lincoln.

His well-known work, "The Puritan," was erected in Springfield, Massachusetts. This statue is a memorial to Deacon Chapin, the puritan, who was one of the founders of Springfield. It is said that his son posed for the figure, which was later presented to his native city. The statue is not, as is often supposed, a portrait, but instead this bronze figure has become a medium through which is expressed the fundamental traits always associated with puritan character.

Among the sculptor's last works is the Sherman statue which today stands on Fifth Avenue, at the 59th Street entrance to Central Park, New York. This is considered the finest equestrian sculpture produced by an American.

Saint Gaudens was working on this statue in 1897. The same year he took it to Paris, completed it and had it cast. The year of the great Paris Exposition was at hand. He sent in his completed model. It was hailed as a masterpiece and given the place of honor at the exhibition. The sculptor, also, was presented with the highest distinctions by the French people. In view of this it is not surprising that he wrote home saying; "I have acquired a strange feeling of confidence that I never felt before, together with a respect for what we are doing at home, in fact, I shall return a red-hot patriot."

The three greatest equestrian statues of the world are: the "Gattamalata," in Padua, by Donatello; the "Colleoni," in Venice by Verrochio; and "General Sherman" in New York City, by Saint Gaudens.

Augustus Saint Gaudens stands at the very pinnacle of American sculpture. His works are many. The distinction of the "Lincoln" is, however, typical of all. Each is a wonderful conception of American character idealized in portrait.

STUDY FOR APPRECIATION

1. What is the sculptor's chief interest in portraiture?
   How does he express these ideas?

2. The pose of Lincoln's figure brings certain lines into prominence. What are they?
   What do lines of this type suggest?

3. What characteristics of Lincoln are expressed by this kind of line?

4. Name other qualities, and tell how each is suggested in the figure.

5. Does the chair add to the design?
   Has the sculptor shown any relation between figure and chair?

6. How has the sculptor secured fine art form in his design?

7. Who is the artist?
   How does he rank among sculptors?

8. Make a sketch showing the structural lines of the composition.

9. Name several famous works of this master.

Related Music: LARGO ...._Handel_
INVICTUS..................... _Bruno Huhn_
KELLER'S AMERICAN HYMN
Keller

LEADERS IN AMERICAN ART

The honor roll of American art is long and illustrious. Inness, Whistler, Sargent, Homer, Thayer, Duveneck, Bellows, Alexander, and Saint Gaudens are brilliant lights in the constellation of American art. With these men, however, are associated the names of others who have also achieved great distinction. Each is distinguished in his own field, whether it be portrait and figure painting, landscape, marine painting, mural decoration, or sculpture. The following pages are dedicated to those men and women whose work is a genuine and permanent contribution to the aesthetic development of America.

BENJAMIN WEST
(1738-1820)

The name of Benjamin West is first in every survey of American art. He is our first native painter. That a child born and reared in the primitive environment of a Pennsylvania village, and in the austere atmosphere of a Quaker home should become a leader in the art world of two hemispheres is indeed phenomenal. Such, however, is the record of Benjamin West.

Benjamin West's grandfather came to America with William Penn. The West family settled in Springfield, Pennsylvania, and there

125

in 1738, Benjamin was born. There was little in this pioneer region to nourish genius of any kind. Fortune, however, began to smile upon the child from the first. In after years he laughingly styled himself a "Son of Destiny," and indeed his rapid rise to a most exalted place in his profession reads like a romance.

With the first suggestions of budding genius, a far-seeing uncle declared that "this talent must be fostered." He took the lad to Philadelphia where he could receive instruction and at the same time view the work of other artists. While there an eminent educator, thrilled by his genius, helped him through college and assisted him in his art studies. Later the lad went to New York, where in a short time he became a full-fledged portrait painter.

At this time in our colonial history the great portrait painters of England were flourishing —Reynolds, Romney and Gainsborough. They exerted a powerful influence upon our early painters. For this reason the beginnings of American art lie largely in the field of figure and portrait painting.

In 1786, when twenty-two years old, West was invited to share passage with a friend sailing for Italy. Arriving there he was introduced as "the young artist from America." Sir Joshua Reynolds and Thomas Gainsborough later formed a warm friendship for the young

American. He was soon brought to the attention of the king, George III. He became a favorite and was made court-painter to His Majesty.

It was during the reign of George III in 1786 and through the influence of West that the Royal Academy of London was founded. Sir Joshua Reynolds, the first president, was succeeded by Benjamin West, who held the honor the remainder of his life.

Aside from his fame as a fashionable portrait painter, West's name is always associated with his historical picture, "The Death of Wolfe." In this painting the artist departed from all previous standards in the matter of costume. Instead of a classic drapery, which was the established form, he chose to dress his figures in the type of costume that was actually worn. So revolutionary was this idea that it was well nigh intolerable to the leading critics of the day. Shortly after the completion of the picture Sir Joshua Reynolds called at the studio to view it. After careful study he turned to the painter and seizing him by both hands, exclaimed: "You have conquered, West! I retract my objections. The picture is painted as it ought to be painted. I foresee that this picture will not only become one of the most popular, but will occasion a revolution in art." This prophecy has been abundantly fulfilled.

Since that time all historical paintings, as well as sculpture, present the character in costume true to the period.

America will honor the name and record of Benjamin West, the painter who led the way for the development of art in the new world.

JOHN SINGLETON COPLEY
(1737-1815)

Among the highly prized paintings of early America is the family portrait group of John Singleton Copley. This painting hangs in the Boston Museum of Fine Arts. Here one sees the artist, an "elegant looking man," his beautiful wife, and his children. The elegance so manifest in this family group is a distinguishing characteristic of all Copley portraits.

John Singleton Copley was contemporary with Benjamin West. Both rose to fame about the same time. Copley was the older of the two. West, however, was the first to receive recognition. Copley was born in Boston in 1737. He received his early training from his step-father, Peter Pelham, who was an artist of some ability. Pelham taught the lad the art of engraving, which in that day was second only to that of artist. The precise hand and careful work of the engraver is a peculiar quality seen in all of Copley's work.

When seventeen Copley received recognition as an artist. Copley and West were warm friends. Upon the advice of the latter, Copley decided to make his residence in England, where success came to him in ever widening channels. His many portraits of the famous men and women of his day have long established him as a painter of rare merit, and placed him among the foremost artists of colonial America.

GILBERT STUART
(1755-1828)

Gilbert Stuart has passed into history as "the painter of presidents." His name is most familiarly associated with the three portraits of George Washington: the Gibbs-Channing portrait of the Metropolitan Museum; the Lansdowne full length portrait in England; and the Athenaeum portrait, in the Boston Museum of Fine Arts, which is most widely known.

Gilbert Stuart is considered the greatest of early American portrait painters. His unusual talent was much in evidence as a child. At thirteen he had received a commission for two portraits. These no doubt were boyish performances, but at least showed the kindly interest of friends in the lad's apparent genius. His talent later attracted a Scotch physician, who took the boy to Scotland for study. He then went to London, where he entered the studio of Benjamin West, the staunch friend of all struggling American artists. After several years with this great master, he set up a studio of his own in London. Here he lived in grand style, for success came to him early. It is said that Stuart never painted a portrait unless the character and personality of the subject pleased him. In 1792, his fame established, he returned to his native land to paint the portrait of that first great American, President Washington. Today this is his most celebrated work.

ALEXANDER H. WYANT
(1836-1892)

In the story of American landscape painting Alexander Wyant occupies an important place. Wyant, George Inness, and Homer Martins have been named the "fathers of American landscape."

Following the great vogue for portrait painting which occupied our colonial artists came a period of American landscape painting. The earlier landscape painters aimed for realistic and grandiose representations of nature. It was many years before it came to be understood that the ART in landscape painting lies in the WAY it is painted. The gradual change from the realistic representation of a scene to the INTERPRETATION OF MOOD covered a long period of growth. Among the leaders who were able to select choice elements in a nature setting, compose them into a picture, and paint them in masses rather than in detail, were the three famous artists, Alexander Wyant, George Inness*, and Homer Martins.

Alexander Wyant was born in 1836, in Defiance, Ohio. As a child he readily expressed himself with brush and pencil. He drew and painted objects that interested him long before he had the opportunity for study or for seeing the work of other artists. In fact, he taught himself to draw. It was not until he was twenty years old that he saw his first pictures.

He happened to be in Cincinnati during an exhibition of paintings. It is said that he studied the pictures "hungrily." He selected the one he liked best. It proved to be one by George Inness. So inspired and stimulated was he by this picture that he decided to pack up his little sketches and take them to Mr. Inness for the sole purpose of asking "whether he might dare to hope to become an artist."

Mr. Inness had experienced many similar calls. He looked over the drawings and advised the young man to go on with his art.

Wyant followed the advice of Mr. Inness, studying both in this country and in Europe.

* See page 26.

His great inspirations were the English artists, Turner and Constable, and his fellow countryman, George Inness, who became one of his most cherished friends.

Mr. Wyant experienced many hardships. Never robust in health, his right side gradually became paralyzed, and with this he lost the use of his right arm. Then it was that the left hand was called upon to do his work. It is said that the pictures of this period excelled those of the earlier date.

Wyant was of a poetic temperament. He has been called the "lyric poet-painter." His pictures have been likened to "musical lyrics in a minor key."

HOMER MARTINS
(1836-1897)

Homer Martins was a member of that famous group, Wyant, Inness, and Martins, the leaders of modern landscape in America.

Strange as it may seem, it was adversity that placed Mr. Martins in this foremost role. Suffering from defective eyesight, it was impossible for him to see details—to visualize clearly the outlines of forms in nature. In short, it was the IMPRESSION of a scene which he recorded. He was the first of our American artists to paint in this manner independently.

Mr. Martins underestimated his own work

because he could not see nature as did other artists of his day. After he had visited France, however, and had become acquainted with Corot and other of the Barbizon artists, he began to see that the impression of a scene, the pattern of the masses softened against the sky, was far more interpretative than a realistic representation.

It is said that the artist would sit for hours with half-closed eyes, smoking, apparently doing nothing. He was, however, absorbing the scene before him. Later it gradually took form in his mind, and subsequently he painted his picture.

Among his best known paintings are: "The Harp of the Winds," in the Metropolitan Museum; "The Fire Worshippers" and "Winchester Hills," both in private collections.

WILLIAM MORRIS HUNT
(1829-1879)

It is said that William Morris Hunt did more than any other man during the sixties and seventies "to improve American painting and American taste." He was a great teacher to whom many of his contemporaries paid grateful tribute.

Unlike many of the world's great painters, William Morris Hunt was never "a struggling artist." From the first every advantage was his,—education, culture, and wealth. As a young man he left Harvard University, going to Rome to begin the study of sculpture. While there, however, he changed his mind and decided that he wanted to become a painter. He soon took up his residence in Paris, where he began seriously the study of painting.

It was while in Paris that he visited an exhibition of the pictures of Millet, the French painter of peasant life. He was greatly charmed with this painter's style. Though at this time Millet's art was not taken seriously, and indeed was often ridiculed, Hunt took a decided stand in the artist's favor. He planned to visit Millet, and become better acquainted with the man and his art. Accordingly he journeyed to Barbizon, a short distance from Paris, and there found Millet and a group of painters who were known as "the progressives." Instead of following the older classic idea that only perfect beauty was worthy of being painted, they found beauty in simple bits of wayside scenery and in the simple life of the working people about them. They emphasized the selection of ESSENTIALS in a picture rather than photographic representation. It was here that Hunt found the very thing for which he was looking. He remained with them for three years.

Upon his return to America in 1855, he

brought with him a number of Millet canvases. In these pictures the lowly, laborious life of the French peasant had been glorified! Millet had chosen only the essentials for his pictures, and painted them in broad simple planes. These pictures were "living witnesses" to Hunt's theory. He insisted that the merit of a picture lies not in the subject but in the painter's interpretation. He insisted upon ESSENTIALS and that they be painted simply. It was this message of essentials and common things made beautiful through simplicity of interpretation, that was his message to America. This was the contribution of the Barbizon painters to American art.

Mr. Hunt has left a number of well known works. One of the most delightful is "The Bathers," in the Worcester Art Museum. In this painting he has expressed the spirit of sport in as fine and simple a way as did Millet the spirit of toil.

JOHN LA FARGE.
(1835-1910)

In every story of American painting the name of John La Farge fills a very important place. He is one of America's great men in the field of the arts. He was both artist and scientist, a rare combination. Yet it was just this combination that made possible the unusual career of John La Farge, and his many and varied contributions to American art.

La Farge was a painter of flowers, landscape, and figures. He excelled in the field of ideal figures. He was a colorist, a mural decorator, a designer of stained-glass windows. His was the genius that evolved the rare beauty of stained-glass effects. He was a critic, a lecturer, and a writer on art subjects.

Born in New York in 1835, John La Farge grew up planning to go into the active business world. There must have been something, of which he was dimly conscious, which drew him toward the art field, for he said: "No one struggled more against this destiny than I." Finally after finishing his university training, he decided to familiarize himself with the meaning and technique of art. This was not, however, with any idea of becoming an artist, but simply that his understanding of the subject might be increased and thus his appreciation developed. Accordingly when twenty-one he went to Paris to carry out this intention.

Seeking a well known French master of that day, he made known his plans. The teacher was not particularly sympathetic with the young man's idea, but consented to aid him. He advised him above all else to study in the galleries by copying the works of the great masters. This La Farge proceeded to do.

Through this practice he became critically interested in color and color effects. Among his other attainments it is as a colorist that Mr. La Farge has been eminently honored.

The first painting of the artist to attract attention was a figure of St. Paul designed for a church decoration. Though the work was not accepted, it drew so much favorable comment that it proved the beginning of a long line of brilliant examples of church decorations for which he is now famous.

It is not surprising that these figures designed for churches led the artist's interest into the wider field of mural decoration. Accordingly, when Trinity Church, Boston, was completed, his first opportunity was presented. He was invited to plan the interior decoration. This was practically his pioneer work in mural painting. It proved to be the most important wall decoration that had been done thus far in America.

This commission was followed rapidly by others. The artist's greatest mural painting is conceded to be "The Ascension of our Lord," in the Church of the Ascension, New York City.

The artist's work in mural decoration gradually unfolded another line of thought. He began to see that the color harmonies of his interiors were greatly influenced by the colored glass of the windows. He consequently turned his attention to the making of colored glass, and finally worked out a kind of glass called "opaline glass." He found that by using glass of different thicknesses and with varying surface and opalescent effects, he was able to produce the beautiful tones seen in the rare glass of the old cathedrals. John La Farge is preeminently the American designer of stained glass windows.

One of the artist's most beautiful windows is the "Watson Memorial" in Trinity Church, Buffalo, New York; another is "The Battle Window," Harvard University; and still another is the "Peacock Window" in the Art Museum, Worcester, Massachusetts.

La Farge was remarkably versatile, turning with the greatest ease from one form of artistic expression to another,—figure painting, landscape, mural painting, designing of stained-glass windows, work in oils, pastels, or water colors. His extensive travels, observations and study enabled him to make a lasting contribution to his own day, and also to succeeding generations.

ELIHU VEDDER.
(1836-1923)

Elihu Vedder was distinctly a creative artist. His originality, the character and quality of his imagination, and his decorative power in expressing his ideas, have made him a unique figure in American painting.

Strange as it may seem, Mr. Vedder cared very little for the painting of landscape for itself, or for the play of light and shade upon form. His art is not the objective art. It is always an idea symbolic. His interest lay in the PATTERN given to his idea, and these patterns were always highly decorative. All through his art runs a strange, a sometimes weird note. He was frequently called "The mystic of no country but his own." He says that a mystery explained is a mystery destroyed, and since he himself cannot explain certain mysteries, he can only represent them as they appear to him.

Though Mr. Vedder was born in New York City, he went to Paris when twenty years of age, and thence to Rome, in which city he made his permanent home. It was not until 1884 that the artist became generally known in his own country. At that time he had illustrated a translation of the Persian poem, the RUBAI-YAT. When this was published it occasioned widespread admiration. "Never before," said a critic, had a book of poems received a pictorial commentary so sympathetic, so beautiful and so illuminative."

Since that time he has become more widely

known, both for his easel pictures and his mural paintings. His unusual gift of original and creative thought, combined with his power for decorative treatment in line and mass, has given him high rank among our American artists.

Among his pictures the "Head of Lazarus", "The Lair of the Serpent", and "The Sphinx" in the Boston Museum of Fine Arts have created general comment. "Keeper of the Threshold" in the Carnegie Institute, Pittsburgh, is another painting strong in decorative treatment and charged with that weird power characteristic of the artist.

Mr. Vedder's first mural work was a decoration for the wall and ceiling of a private residence in New York City. This was so highly successful that the following year he was called upon for a decorative panel for the Memorial Art Building on the campus of Bowdoin College. Then followed the artist's best known mural work,—the five panels and the one mosaic, "Minerva", in the Library of Congress, Washington, D. C. These paintings take their place perfectly upon the stone walls.

Mr. Vedder stands in a place apart. His work is peculiarly his own,—a thoroughly individual and thoroughly independent contribution to our national art.

WILLIAM MERRITT CHASE.
(1849-1916)

William Merritt Chase is recognized not only as one of America's distinguished painters, but also as one of the greatest teachers in American art. In fact his reputation as a teacher began shortly after his student days in Europe. From that time on his work in this field continued. So unceasing was his devotion to hundreds of students, and so grateful were they to their teacher, that as a testimonial of their great regard they invited John Singer Sargent to paint his portrait. The painting was then presented to the Metropolitan Museum of Art. This painting is regarded as one of the great portraits in the collection of the Museum.

Hastily reviewing Mr. Chase's teaching record, we find him on his return to New York City in 1878 beginning his work in the Art Students' League. Here he remained for eighteen years. In 1897 the Chase School of Art was organized in New York City. This school was one of the powerful influences of that day. Later it became the New York School of Fine and Applied Arts. Mr. Chase also taught in the Pennsylvania Academy of Fine Arts, and in the Art School at Hartford, Connecticut. During many summers he conducted students' classes abroad, and later he established a summer school, "Art Colony", on Long Island. In view of this unusual record it is not surprising that he is known today as the "Great Teacher of the East."

When a young man of nineteen Mr. Chase began studying art in Indianapolis, where he lived. He later attended the National Academy of Design. His first studio was opened in St. Louis, where he hoped to become a full-fledged portrait painter. In those days, however, he found people more interested and willing to pay for pictures of fruits and flowers than for portraits. These still life studies were painted in very realistic fashion, with a careful attention to detail.

By and by in the early seventies we find young Chase on his way to Munich. This artistic city of Germany was now sharing honors with Paris as a center for art students. Here Mr. Chase found a whole colony of American students, among them the great teacher, Frank Duveneck.*

Mr. Chase's work in Munich brought him many honors which finally led to the offer of a professorship in the Royal Academy of Munich. After serious consideration the flattering offer was declined, and Mr. Chase decided to share his honors with his native land. In after years, referring to this decision, he said

* See page 47

simply: "I was young. America was young. I had faith in it."

In 1878 the artist returned to America, and began his long and busy career as teacher in the Students' Art League of New York City. Mr. Chase brought so much enthusiasm to his work and profoundly influenced so large a group of students, that he is everywhere not only famous as a great painter, but is also recognized as having been a most conspicuous and beneficent force in American schools of art.

Though Mr. Chase painted both portraits and landscape he is best known for his still life subjects, and especially those in which fish are conspicuous. He took special delight in painting fish, and this was always superbly done. The story is told that in England the artist once rented a fine cod for two hours, took it to his room and painted it. This picture was purchased by the Corcoran Gallery of Art, Washington, D. C., for two thousand dollars. The venture having proved so profitable, Chase offered the fishmonger more money for his former loan. The man was unwilling to accept more, but winking at Mr. Chase he replied whimsically; "It were a good portrait, to be sure, but were it not a fine cod?"

A few of the artist's famous portraits are

those of James McNeill Whistler, Metropolitan Museum of Art; the portrait of his wife, known as the "Lady in a White Shawl", Pennsylvania Academy of Fine Arts; the portrait of his daughter, "Alice", in the Art Institute of Chicago.

America is grateful for the confidence that led Mr. Chase to cast his fortune with his native land. His faith is abundantly rewarded.

EDWIN HOWLAND BLASHFIELD.
(1848-1936)

Among the conspicuous American painters who have exerted a highly constructive influence on American development in the arts, is Edwin Howland Blashfield. Not alone as artist, but as traveler, lecturer, and author, he has added immeasurably to the meaning of art in America.

Mr. Blashfield's name is usually associated with his inspiring mural decorations. He has painted the wall decorations in many of our state capital buildings. The most imposing of these is in the Capitol at Madison, Wisconsin. In the Library of Congress is his greatest decoration, entitled "Human Understanding and the Progress of Civilization." As recently as 1926 Mr. Blashfield completed the four mosaic panels representing the four evangelists, in St. Matthew's Roman Catholic Church, in Washington, D. C.

As a young man of eighteen Mr. Blashfield followed the advice of William Morris Hunt and went abroad to study. His work in both Paris and London was highly honored. After fifteen years of foreign study and travel, he returned to America to continue in his chosen field. Through his lectures, his writings, and as president of the Royal Academy of Design, he has exercised a lasting influence upon American art.

CHILDE HASSAM.
(1859-1935)

Childe Hassam represents the new influence which came to American art in the eighties. This new influence came direct from the impressionists in France. These painters believed that instead of a literal representation of a scene only the impression should be recorded. Hence they were called "IMPRESSIONISTS."

As the impressionist movement grew, sunlight and color became of prime importance. Brilliant effects were obtained by placing small spots of pure color side by side upon the canvas. Viewed from a distance these colors blended and produced a far more sparkling effect than when mixed. Childe Hassam is the

American apostle of sunlight and pure color!

Mr. Hassam was born in Boston, and was educated in the Boston public schools. Here he had his earliest instruction in drawing. He says: "I remember even as a little shaver I showed enough proficiency to be selected by the teacher to decorate the blackboards." Later he attended the Boston Art School. In 1886 he went to France, where he came under the direct influence of the impressionists.

Upon his return to America in 1866 he made his home in New York City. Here he continued to live and work. Mr. Hassam considers the streets of New York "the most beautiful in the world," and indeed he has made them famous.

His New York street scenes, streets flooded with sunlight or drenched in rain, are never real streets but the poetic expression of the light and atmosphere that envelop them. Among them are "Washington Arch," "Spring, Madison Square", and "Union Square." During the World War, Mr. Hassam painted these streets gay with bunting and flags for "Allies Day." This is one of the great pictures of that period.

The artist is likewise interested in interiors, and the play of light and color through a window. He likes to place a figure near a curtained window with flowers and other objects near by, and then paint the bright sparkling sunlight without, the light within, and the reflected lights in the furnishings. Among his pictures of this type are "The Strawberry Tea Set", and "The Gold Fish Window."

Mr. Hassam's outdoor scenes are vibrant with this same light and color. Clumps of green trees, fields, streams of rippling water, and old buildings sparkling white in the sunlight, hold a fascination for him. The "Church of Old Lyme", in the Albright Gallery, Buffalo, is an excellent example of an outdoor picture painted in the impressionistic manner.

"Why should not one be an impressionist", he challenges. Is not all nature revealed to us in this manner? We must reproduce only what we see and as we see it."

MARY CASSATT.
(1855-1926)

Among American women painters the late Mary Cassatt has achieved great distinction. Miss Cassatt is contemporary with Childe Hassam, Robert Weir, John H. Twachtman, and other leading impressionists of American birth.

Miss Cassatt lived most of her life in Paris. Though as a child she had studied at the Pennsylvania Academy of Fine Arts, it was in the galleries of Italy, Spain, and Flanders that she received her first deep impressions. Here she studied the great old masters, particularly Corregio and Rubens, imbibing so much of their style that for many years her work showed this influence.

As Miss Cassatt continued her studies her work became more widely recognized, and she was admitted to the Paris Salon. Along in the eighties the impressionists were gradually coming into favor. One of their leaders, the famous Degas, was one day walking through the gallery, when he stopped before one of Miss Cassatt's pictures. After studying it for some time, he said with emphasis; "That is genuine. There is one who sees as I do." Soon after he invited Miss Cassatt to exhibit with the impressionist group. She was delighted. "Already," she said, "I had recognized who were my masters. I admired Monet, Courbet, and Degas. I hated conventional art. Now I began to live." From the time that Miss Cassatt began to exhibit with the impressionist group she became known as an impressionist.

Miss Cassat's pictures are different in subject from those of other painters of this group. She is famous for pictures of mothers and children. These pictures are usually posed in full sunlight. The figures are superbly drawn, and the subjects never spoiled by the trivial addition of pretty clothes and ornament. It is said that few men artists equal her "mother and child pictures. Her great friend, Degas, upon viewing a superb Cassatt picture remarked with great emphasis: "I will not admit that a woman can draw like that." Miss Cassatt's technique is always simple, strong, and direct, whether working in oils, pastels, dry point, or colored etchings.

In 1914 the Pennsylvania Academy of Fine Arts, the school in which she began her studies, presented her with a gold medal. In 1927, the year following her death, a memorial exhibition of her work was held at the Academy. Today her pictures are found in the leading museums of the country.

Though Miss Cassatt lived most of her life abroad, she was emphatic upon one point,—that she was "thoroughly American."

CECELIA BEAUX.
(1863-1942)

Among American painters Cecelia Beaux holds a coveted place. In 1926 her high position in American portraiture was recognized by two distinguished institutions, which awarded her honors of national significance. The Academy of Arts and Letters presented her with the gold medal of the Academy. This she received in "recognition of a talent which during a long career of unremitting effort has never fallen below a very high plane." The second honor was the invitation from the Italian Minister of Public Instruction to place a self-portrait in the Ufizzi Gallery, Florence. This is a very distinguished honor, for in this gallery hang only the portraits of the great masters of all time.

When twenty-two years old Miss Beaux received her first recognition,—a prize of one hundred dollars which had been offered for the best picture painted by a resident of Philadelphia. In 1885, 1891, and 1892 she won the same prize.

In viewing the development of Miss Beaux's art it is easily seen that her earliest trend is painting the portraits of women and children. She painted these with the greatest sympathy, imparting to her canvas the charm and loveliness which she found in her subjects. With the maturity of her art, we find later many impressive portraits of men. Among these paintings none are greater than the three portraits of World War heroes which she was commissioned to paint for the National Gallery at Washington, D. C.,—portraits of Clemenceau, Cardinal Mercier, and Admiral Beatty.

It is said that the artist sat in a visitor's box during the sessions at Versailles, looking down upon the rugged "tiger" as he delivered his impassioned addresses from the tribune. The impression which the great statesman made at that time lives again in the famous portrait which now hangs in Washington.

In the portrait of Cardinal Mercier, who posed frequently for the artist, one detects the kindly and heroic traits which so enthralled the painter. The dauntless personality of Admiral Beatty is vigorously expressed in his portrait. Each of these portraits shows the power of the artist in seizing upon manifest characteristics, and her sure, firm hand in execution.

Among Miss Beaux's most celebrated paintings is "The Dancing Lesson," Chicago Art Institute, showing the children of Richard Watson Gilder going through the rhythmic steps of the dance. Miss Beaux herself regards this picture as one of the finest she has done. Such is a portion, only, of the distinguished record of one of America's foremost women painters.

VIOLET OAKLEY.
(1874-1961)

In the annals of American art three women have attained great distinction,—Mary Cassatt, Cecelia Beaux, and Violet Oakley. So exceptional is the work of these three artists that they hold an eminent place among our great American painters.

Miss Oakley's field is distinctly that of the mural painter. It was after the untimely death of the distinguished mural painter, Edwin

Austin Abbey, who had partly completed his great decoration in the State Capitol, Harrisburg, Pa., that Miss Oakley was selected to finish the work. This was the first time, in this or any other country, that a commission so important had been entrusted to a woman. This great monument, however, is only one of the many achievements upon which her fame rests.

Miss Oakley began her career as an illustrator. She possessed in marked degree the happy faculty of adjusting figures to a space, and further her work showed great decorative quality. Both these qualities are essential to successful mural decoration. It is not surprising, therefore, that at the age of twenty-four she received a commission for five stained-glass window designs and several mural decorations for the Church of All Saints, New York City. They were so successful that a few years later she was invited to design the murals for the governor's reception room in the Pennsylvania Capitol. These murals are particularly expressive of Miss Oakley's creative power. She chooses historical events and clothes them with a vision peculiarly her own. These panels are so arranged that they form a frieze six feet high about the upper part of the room. The theme, "The Founding of the State of Liberty Spiritual", pictures the early history of Pennsylvania, the activities of William Penn, the record of Quaker thought, and leads to the final triumph,—the signing of the charter of Pennsylvania. Following this the artist was given the commission for the large mural, "The Constitutional Convention," in the courthouse in Cleveland.

Having accomplished so much in successful mural work, Miss Oakley was exceptionally prepared for the great honor which came to her in being selected to complete the work in the Pennsylvania State House. Mr. Abbey had left no designs, consequently the decoration as it stands today is wholly the expression of Miss Oakley's creative imagination. Here as always Miss Oakley is the illustrator, not only of historical facts, but as well of her own ideas and ideals. This great monument of nine panels, aside from its inspirational quality, is historical and informative in the highest degree in relation to the period in whch the events occurred. They remain "the crowning glory of the art treasures of Pennsylvania," and a permanent monument to the artist.

FREDERIC REMINGTON.

Among American painters of the Great West Frederic Remington was the first to bring to the East the color, life, and action of the western plains. His Indians, cowboys, and bucking broncos are graphic recordings of a life that has now all but vanished.

Mr. Remington's early work as an illustrator proved a preparation for his later work as painter. His ability to sketch rapidly trained his eye for that swift, exciting movement which was so characteristic of the West of thirty years ago. As one writer says: "His horses move as if on springs. Their heels play like lightning over the earth. You feel them hurling themselves into the hunt, going nervously into action at the crack of bullets."

As a painter Mr. Remington continued to be the illustrator, translating into pictorial forms the color, life, and adventure of the West. As a sculptor he also gained distinction. His several equestrian bronzes are fully as picturesque and spirited as his pictures. "The Cowboy," a characteristic work, has been erected in Fairmount Park, Philadelphia.

Though today many of our well known painters are finding the color and life of the West an inspiring subject for their talents, to Frederic Remington belongs the precedence of the pioneer in this distinctive field.

DANIEL CHESTER FRENCH.
(1850-1931)

It is said that three men have guided the destinies of American sculpture for the past forty years,—John Quincy Adams Ward, Augustus Saint Gaudens, and Daniel Chester French.

The work of Mr. Ward now ranks highest among that of our early sculptors. Saint Gaudens* is our greatest sculptor. Daniel Chester French, the youngest of the trio, was next after Saint Gaudens to be awarded the gold medal of the National Institute of Arts and Letters. This honor places him in the forefront of modern American sculptors.

It seems incredible that a youth of twenty-three, with only a month's instruction to his credit and a few lectures on anatomy, could produce a work of art worthy of the name. Yet this is the record of Mr. French. The particular piece of work accomplished was "The Minute Man," which today marks the historic spot in Concord, Mass., where in 1775 the British first met the fire of Colonial troops.

After the recognition of this, his first important work, Mr. French spent a year in Florence, in the studio of Thomas Ball, the American. Upon his return to this country many commissions came to him. His most notable work at this time is the fine portrait bust of Emerson. He later developed more imaginative tendencies, and we find among the works of this period the "Gallaudet Memorial," in Washing-

---

* See page 119.

ton, and the Milmore monument, "Death and the Sculptor." This is one of the most widely admired works of the sculptor.

It was in the Columbian Exposition in Chicago, in 1893, that a new trend developed in Mr. French's art,—i. e., sculpture in relation to architecture. His colossal single figure, "Statue of the Republic," seen as an isolated figure was scarcely beautiful, but placed in its architectural setting it became the imposing center of the whole architectural scheme. Other famous works of a similar character are the "Alma Mater," which has been placed in the center of the landing, half way up the stairs leading to the Library of Columbia University, and the colossal bronze seated figure of Lincoln, enshrined within the Lincoln Memorial at Washington. This figure, unveiled in 1923, is considered the greatest work of the artist.

Mr. French is said to be the most classic of American sculptors. It is indeed true that he has enveloped these great creations with that serenity which we know as "classic."

Other famous works of the sculptor are the "Alice Freeman Palmer Memorial," and the bronze doors of the Boston Public Library.

As a tribute to his distinguished achievements in the field of sculpture, the National Sculpture Society, in 1927, presented Mr. French with the Society's first medal of honor.

TO THE TEACHER

A study of the world's masterpieces of painting and sculpture in the high school aims to develop not only pleasure and interest in the beautiful, but as well an intelligent understanding of that which makes for beauty, i.e. an understanding of the ART FORM of these masterpieces.

It is all very well to like pictures, to enjoy them; but for intelligent appreciation of their beauty something more, something of those qualities which go to make a work of art, must be understood. Such an understanding develops a consciousness of ART FORM. To approach this understanding of a masterpiece is to gain in appreciation.

Real appreciation is a combination of the emotional and the intellectual. When only the emotional reaction is considered, appreciation is superficial; when only the intellectual, it becomes mechanical, cold. In the earlier years the enjoyment of little children is purely emotional. With the growing years more of the simpler forms of art structure may be pointed out, while in the high school the emphasis should be placed upon the important elements of ART FORM.

COLOR, LINE, DARK AND LIGHT PATTERN, these are the tools, plus inspiration, which the artist uses to express beauty.

By the fine choices he makes in color, line, and arrangement of dark and light, he succeeds. The possibilities of choice and arrangement are infinite; witness the great number of masterpieces in the world, no two alike. It is this intelligent appreciation of ART STRUCTURE, added to the mere emotional appeal, that is REAL APPRECIATION. It is this more complete understanding of a work of art that imparts increased interest to the study of masterpieces in the high school.

CLASS ROOM PRACTICE.

Before reading any text on a picture, the picture itself should be freely discussed by the class. Pupils should be encouraged to give their own impressions; tell what they like and WHY they like it. Much of the pupil's ability to see will depend on previous study of pictures in the grades. If, as is very possible, the simplest elements in picture making have been previously pointed out, the teacher will find students ready to touch further upon the art form of the picture, discussing color, light and shade, balance, center of interest, and other details.

It is the skilful questioning of the teacher that leads the pupil gradually to discover for himself these elements of design form in picture-making.

All study of painting and sculpture should be done leisurely for enjoyment. It should be a voyage of discovery, a discovery of the fine choices the artist has made in color, line, and pattern in building up his masterpiece.

Suggestions leading to the understanding of CONTENT, ART ELEMENTS, and ART FORM.

I. Content of picture.
      (a) Is picture story-telling?
      (b) Is picture based on nature?
      (c) Is picture imaginative?

II. Art Elements, or Color, Line, Dark and Light.

COLOR.

(a) Note colors used. Are they "warm" or "cold"?
(b) Is color used as in nature?
(c) Is color used to make pattern?
(d) Is color used to give light?
(e) Is color closely related or strongly contrasted?
(f) How does color interpret meaning of picture?
(g) Make color notes matching colors in picture.

LINE.

(a) Is composition based on vertical and horizontal lines?
(b) Is composition based on curved lines?
(c) Is composition based on angular lines?
(d) Is composition based on a combination of all these lines?
(e) Is composition based on pyramidal form?
(f) Trace lines showing composition.

DARK AND LIGHT PATTERN.

(a) Is dark and light used as in nature?
(b) Is dark and light used as in a pattern?
(c) Trace picture massing in dark and light.

III. Art Form or Design.

(a) Does picture show design?
(b) Where is the emphasis?
(c) How is unity secured?
(d) Does artist use color, line, or light and dark pattern to secure unity?
(e) Does he ever use all of these art elements in one picture?

A thoughtful discussion of the foregoing points will lead to an understanding of the art form of any picture.

Since the first appeal in both picture and music is always emotional, the use of music with pictures is to be encouraged. Music, selected for the emotional quality only, leads to an appreciation of the "mood" or "spirit" which the artist has aimed to express. When used in this way, the emotional elements of the two great arts are co-ordinated and appreciated, the one expressed through musical tone, the other through fine choices in color, line, and pattern.

True, indeed, is it that the arts have much in common. An appreciation of art form in painting and sculpture provides the student with a background for the intelligent appreciation of all the fine arts.

www.ingramcontent.com/pod-product-compliance
Lightning Source LLC
Chambersburg PA
CBHW051213090426
42742CB00021B/3433